The Thirteen Colonies

Georgia

The Thirteen Colonies

Georgia

Christina M. Girod

Lucent Books, Inc.
P.O. Box 289011, San Diego, California

Library of Congress Cataloging-in-Publication Data

Girod, Christina M.
  Georgia / by Christina M. Girod
    p. cm. — (The Thirteen colonies)
  Includes bibliographical references and index.
  Summary: Provides a history of Georgia, from the struggles between Native Americans and Europeans to control this land of military and economic importance, to its becoming the fourth state of the Union.
    ISBN 1-56006-990-2 (hardback : alk. paper)
    1. Georgia—History—Colonial period, ca. 1600–1775—Juvenile literature. 2. Georgia—History—1775–1865—Juvenile literature. [1. Georgia—History—Colonial period, ca. 1600–1775. 2. Georgia—History—1775–1865.] I. Title II. Thirteen colonies (Lucent Books)
    F289 .G53 2002
    975.8'02—dc21

                                                                    2001002786

Contents

Foreword

T he story of the thirteen English colonies that became the United States of America is one of startling diversity, conflict, and cultural evolution. Today, it is easy to assume that the colonists were of one mind when fighting for independence from England and afterwards when the national government was created. However, the American colonies had to overcome a vast reservoir of distrust rooted in the broad geographical, economic, and social differences that separated them. Even the size of the colonies contributed to the conflict; the smaller states feared domination by the larger ones.

These sectional differences stemmed from the colonies' earliest days. The northern colonies were more populous and their economies were more diverse, being based on both agriculture and manufacturing. The southern colonies, however, were dependent on agriculture—in most cases, the export of only one or two staple crops. These economic differences led to disagreements over things such as the trade embargo the Continental Congress imposed against England during the war. The southern colonies wanted their staple crops to be exempt from the embargo because their economies would have collapsed if they could not trade with England, which in some cases was the sole importer. A compromise was eventually made and the southern colonies were allowed to keep trading some exports.

In addition to clashing over economic issues, often the colonies did not see eye to eye on basic political philosophy. For example, Connecticut leaders held that education was the route to greater political liberty, believing that knowledgeable citizens would not allow themselves to be stripped of basic freedoms and rights. South Carolinians, on the other hand, thought that the protection of personal property and economic independence was the basic foundation of freedom. In light of such profound differences it is amazing that the colonies were able to unite in the fight for independence and then later under a strong national government.

Why, then, did the colonies unite? When the Revolutionary War began the colonies set aside their differences and banded together because they shared a common goal—gaining political freedom from what they considered a tyrannical monarchy—that could be more easily attained if they cooperated with each other. However, after the war ended, the states abandoned unity and once again pursued sectional interests, functioning as little nations in a weak confederacy. The congress of this confederacy, which was bound by the Articles of Confederation, had virtually no authority over the individual states. Much bickering ensued— the individual states refused to pay their war debts to the national government, the nation was sinking further into an economic depression, and there was nothing the national government could do. Political leaders realized that the nation was in jeopardy of falling apart. They were also aware that European nations such as England, France, and Spain were all watching the new country, ready to conquer it at the first opportunity. Thus the states came together at the Constitutional Convention in order to create a system of government that would be both strong enough to protect them from invasion and yet nonthreatening to state interests and individual liberties.

The Thirteen Colonies series affords the reader a thorough understanding of how the development of the individual colonies helped create the United States. The series examines the early history of each colony's geographical region, the founding and first years of each colony, daily life in the colonies, and each colony's role in the American Revolution. Emphasis is given to the political, economic, and social uniqueness of each colony. Both primary and secondary quotes enliven the text, and sidebars highlight personalities, legends, and personal stories. Each volume ends with a chapter on how the colony dealt with changes after the war and its role in developing the U.S. Constitution and the new nation. Together, the books in this series convey a remarkable story—how thirteen fiercely independent colonies came together in an unprecedented political experiment that not only succeeded, but endures to this day.

Introduction

Georgia's Legacy

Georgia had perhaps the most unique beginning of all the English colonies established in America. However, despite the fact that it was founded to bring hope and new opportunities to oppressed people—in fact, banning slavery and any activity with Native Americans that could be harmful to the natives—Georgia eventually developed a society and economy much like those of the other southern colonies.

Perhaps the most remarkable fact about Georgia is the astounding speed with which the colony's citizens progressed from being "charity colonists," who had no voice in their government, to self-governing and independent citizens of the Revolutionary era—a process that took a mere forty years. The editors of the book *Colonial Georgia* explain this phenomenon:

> During a brief twenty-five-year period under the crown, Georgia experienced much of the history of all the mainland colonies: growing demographic heterogeneity [ethnic diversity], rapid economic development, increasing religious liberality, and the emergence of . . . the Assembly . . . for expressing those principles of self-government that by 1776 were the common property of all the colonies. Georgians, nevertheless, had ample reasons for approaching independence cautiously: they were young, isolated, and defenseless. They chose to follow their northern brethren not so much out of

material interest as out of the conviction that they were more American than British. [1]

Influence of Immigrants

Georgia was also unique in that no dominant ethnic group made up the colony's population. Although it was an English colony, at its

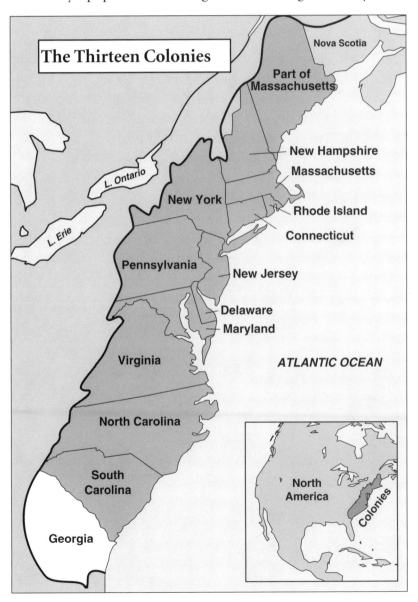

The Thirteen Colonies

Nova Scotia

Part of Massachusetts

New Hampshire

Massachusetts

L. Ontario

New York

Rhode Island

Connecticut

L. Erie

Pennsylvania

New Jersey

Delaware

Maryland

Virginia

ATLANTIC OCEAN

North Carolina

South Carolina

North America

Colonies

Georgia

founding many oppressed peoples from other parts of Europe flocked to this place of hope looking for a brighter future. Colonists came from England, Germany, Scotland, Ireland, Holland, Portugal, France, Switzerland, and the colonies to the north. Neither was there a dominant religion—Jews, Lutherans, Moravians, Congregationalists, Quakers, and Anglicans all settled in the colony, although Anglican became the established church of the colony during the years the royal government (England) held control.

The incredible diversity of cultures and creeds in Georgia gave the colony both benefits and disadvantages. Such a diversified society meant that a wealth of different ideas about politics, economics, and human rights were being interchanged within the population. The experience of accommodating so many conflicting interests was one reason why people in Georgia were able to develop the ability to govern themselves in such a brief time. On the other hand, this diversity also lent itself to constant conflict that created an atmosphere ripe for civil war. The enormous variety of opinions regarding the colonies' independence from England contributed to Georgia's lack of commitment to the Revolutionary cause early in the war, and also led to a great deal of violence among civilians during the later war years.

The Georgia colony as it appeared in 1734.

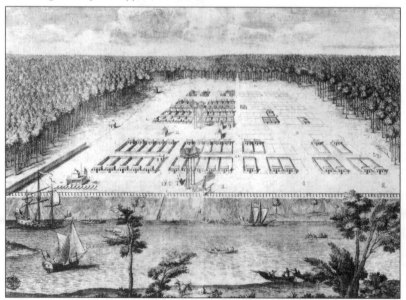

Rise of the Common People and Democracy

After the end of the Revolutionary War, gradually those who had supported England either abandoned Georgia or took oaths of loyalty to the state. Patriots who had supported independence from England during the war became the dominant political faction in Georgia. These frontier people recognized Georgia's great need for protection from invasion by Native Americans and Europeans. As a result there was little controversy over whether or not Georgia would approve the federal Constitution and join the United States.

It is ironic that the philanthropic vision of Georgia's founding—greater economic opportunity and fair and equal rights—eventually changed with the bringing of slavery to the colony. However, the "common people" who were free enjoyed an extraordinary rise of power after the Revolutionary War, leading to a greater degree of democratic authority among free Georgians. The pursuit of democracy, made possible by the failure of aristocracy to take control of the colonial government, is perhaps Georgia's greatest legacy of the colonial era.

Chapter One

Precolonial Times: Conflict and the Struggle to Dominate Georgia

T he earliest years of Georgia's recorded history tell the story of a bitter and sometimes violent struggle among different peoples to dominate the region. Although Native Americans had lived in the region for centuries, after the Europeans' arrival Georgia became the object of a fierce tug-of-war, the highly desired southern military buffer that could protect its controller's interests elsewhere in North America. Spain, England, and to a lesser degree France all vied for control of Georgia at different times, either fighting the natives or recruiting them to fight their two respective European competitors.

Georgia's Earliest Inhabitants

The lush Georgia region was home to several tribes of Native Americans. North of the Savannah River the land was inhabited by the populous Cherokee and a smaller tribe called the Yuchi. The southern part of

Georgia was occupied by the Yamasee and the Hitchiti, small tribes, while the powerful Creek dominated the western and central parts. All but one were Muskogean-speaking—the Cherokee spoke an Iroquois language.

Although the Cherokee were more populous than the Creek, only a small portion of their people lived in Georgia territory. The Creek, who numbered about fifteen thousand, were the primary tribe in the region. Their character and lifestyle were described by James Oglethorpe, who founded the English colony of Georgia, in a letter to England:

> They are a generous good-natured people, very humane to strangers; patient of want and pain; slow to anger, and not easily provoked; but when they are thoroughly incensed, they are implacable [not to be appeased]. . . . Their publick conferences shew [show] them to be men of genius, and they have a natural eloquence. . . . They have no manufactures but what each family makes for its own use; they seem to despise working for hire, and spend their time chiefly in hunting and war; but plant corn enough for the support of their families, and of the strangers that come to visit them. . . .

Fifteen thousand Creek Indians lived in precolonial Georgia.

The land belongs to the women, and the corn that grows upon it; but the meat must be got by the men, because it is they only that hunt. This makes marriage necessary, that the women may furnish corn, and the men meat. [2]

The Creek were actually a group of many Muskogean tribes who had united for their common defense. About fifty self-governing towns made up the Creek confederacy, which formed a formidable barrier against invasion by the Cherokee and their neighbors to the west, the Choctaw. The Creek had no central capital, but they did have a centralized governmental council presided over by a chief, or *micco*. Each town also had its own *micco* who presided over the town council. The *micco* and the council were responsible for making the town laws.

Each town also had several war officials who had earned their position by performing great deeds in battle. These war officials did not participate in the town's civil administration. Rather, they were responsible for the defense of their town or providing military aid to neighboring towns within the confederacy.

The Creek town of homes and storehouses was built around its ceremonial center. This center, called the central square or plaza, held the sacred fire, believed to be a link between people and the Great Spirit. Important meetings, rituals, and ceremonies took place in the plaza, which also served as a place for social gatherings among friends and family.

The residents of each town were divided into clans—groups of people who had a common ancestry. Ancestry was determined matrilineally, which meant it was traced back through the mother to the grandmother and so on. Clan loyalty was stronger than town loyalty. Since people of a single clan lived in many different towns, clan loyalties provided links between communities. However, clan loyalty could also tear towns apart. Feuds between members of different clans could cause divisions between towns or within them. These divisions were fueled by the clan tradition of revenge.

The revenge system was designed to maintain balance and harmony in the spiritual and real worlds. The concept of balance and harmony was central to the Creek way of life. Balance was kept by people replacing anything they took with something of equal value.

For instance, if a woman dug up an herb, she would leave a small token of respect for the herb in its place. A hunter who killed a deer would ask for its forgiveness through prayer. Similarly, if a member of a clan was killed by someone from another clan, the victim's clan killed a person from the killer's clan. Revenge did not have to fall on the murderer, but could be taken out on anyone from the murderer's clan. It did not matter who was killed in revenge because the object was not fairness or justice, but rather restoring the balance between the two clans in order to maintain harmony.

The revenge system, however, was far from perfect. A person from one clan might kill a person from another clan to avenge a death, but then someone from the victim's clan might retaliate by killing someone from the killer's clan. This killing could continue back and forth between the two clans for a long time. If members of both clans lived in the same town. Other clans would also take sides, allying with the clan they were more closely tied to by marriage.

This system later compounded conflicts over land cessions between Native Americans and European settlers. When Indians killed Europeans who settled—sometimes illegally—on their land, the Europeans often retaliated by attacking Indian villages and killing the responsible parties. However, the Indians then would kill any group of settlers, regardless if they were responsible for the previous killing. Europeans did not understand the clan concept of balance and harmony, and saw the revenge system as unfair.

Maintaining balance and harmony in daily work was also important. The Creek were prosperous farmers who grew corn, beans, and squash. They also fished, hunted, and gathered berries, nuts, and other wild fruits. Some Creeks were traders who traveled far to other tribes to barter excess produce, hides, baskets, and other wares. In all these activities the Creek vigilantly maintained a balance between their own needs and the needs of the earth. This system was strictly adhered to until soon after the arrival of the Europeans.

De Soto's Journey Through Georgia

The first European nation to send explorers to the Georgia region was Spain, which first recorded visits to the southeastern part of North America in the early 1500s. In 1539 the Spanish explorer Hernando

In March 1540 Hernando de Soto crossed the Ochlockonee River into Georgia and laid waste to Creek territory.

de Soto arrived in what is now Florida. He led his entourage of six hundred men north toward Georgia, ransacking Native American villages as he went. A Portuguese known as the Gentleman of Elvas described how de Soto treated the natives:

Two captains having been sent in opposite directions, in quest of Indians, a hundred men and women were taken, one or two of whom were chosen out for the Governor [de Soto], as was always customary for themselves and companions. They were led off in chains, with collars about the neck, to carry luggage and grind corn, doing the labor proper to servants.[3]

Around March 1540, de Soto crossed the Ochlockonee River into southwestern Georgia where he encountered the Creek. The Spaniards continued raiding villages and burning crops, and killed and enslaved some of the Creek. Gradually word about the destruction de Soto was creating reached the northern villages of the Creek, the Cherokee, and smaller tribes. Often these villages would be abandoned until de Soto passed them by. At one village, the chief implied that he knew of de Soto's reputation and tried to impress on him that he himself expected better treatment from the Spanish:

Very high, powerful and good master: The things that seldom happen bring astonishment. Think, then, what must be the effect on me and mine, of the sight of you and your people, whom we have at no time seen, astride the fierce brutes, your horses, entering with such speed and fury into my country.

... Trusting to your greatness and personal qualities, I hope no fault will be found in me, and that I shall rather receive favors, of which one is that with my person, my country, and my vassals, you will do as with your own things; another, that you tell me who you are, whence you come, whither you go, and what you seek, that I may the better serve you. [4]

De Soto, however, was not impressed and tried to intimidate the chief by claiming to be a sun god looking for gold. De Soto's reputation eventually prompted many Creek to raid the Spanish expedition in small marauding parties. Eventually de Soto left Georgia, but the expedition ended when he died of disease in 1542.

De Soto's brief journey through Georgia left its mark on the Creek people. They developed a suspicion toward most Europeans and

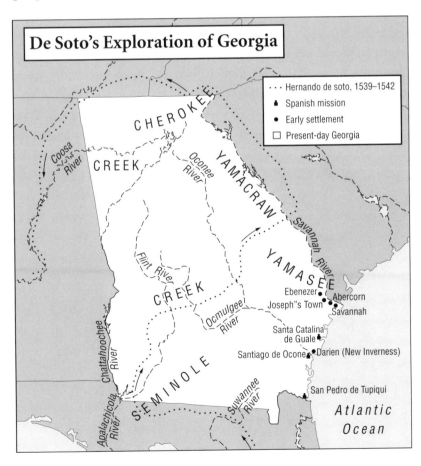

De Soto's Exploration of Georgia

- - - Hernando de soto, 1539–1542
♠ Spanish mission
● Early settlement
□ Present-day Georgia

CHEROKEE

Coosa River

CREEK

Oconee River

YAMACRAW

Savannah River

CREEK

Flint River

YAMASEE

Ebenezer • Abercorn
Joseph"s Town • Savannah

Ocmulgee River

Santa Catalina de Guale ♠

Chattahoochee River

Santiago de Oconee ♠ • Darien (New Inverness)

SEMINOLE

Apalachicola River

Suwannee River

San Pedro de Tupiqui ♠

Atlantic Ocean

many hated and feared them. Nevertheless, as Europeans continued to come to the Georgia region, many Creeks recognized the need to form alliances with them in order to protect themselves against invasion and deceit.

Establishment of the Guale District

Twenty years after de Soto's ill-fated journey, the Spaniards sent Pedro Menendez de Aviles to take control of Florida and Georgia. With fifteen hundred soldiers he intended to protect Spanish claims to the region and prevent invasion by the French or English. Aviles was ordered to establish Spanish forts up and down the coastlines of Florida and Georgia. The first of these forts was built in 1565 at St. Augustine, Florida. The following year a second was erected on St. Catherines Island off the coast of Georgia. Eventually three more forts were constructed on islands off Georgia's coast, and several others were built in the coastal lowlands. (The Spanish called the land between Florida and the English territory to the north—present-day South Carolina—"Guale" after a Native American chief of the same name whom the Spanish befriended on St. Catherines Island.)

The Spanish also hoped to cement claims to the area by establishing church missions along the coast. These missions, mostly Jesuit and Franciscan, attempted to convert the Native Americans to Christianity. The Spanish government also hoped the missions would persuade the Creek and other tribes to form alliances with them against the French and English.

In 1660 Spain sent Pedro Menendez de Aviles with fifteen hundred soldiers to take control of Florida and Georgia.

Spanish Decline in Guale

Despite their establishment of missions and forts on the Georgia coast, the Spanish did little to develop the region beyond religious or military efforts. The absence of an economic base in port towns resulted in Spain's inability to foster

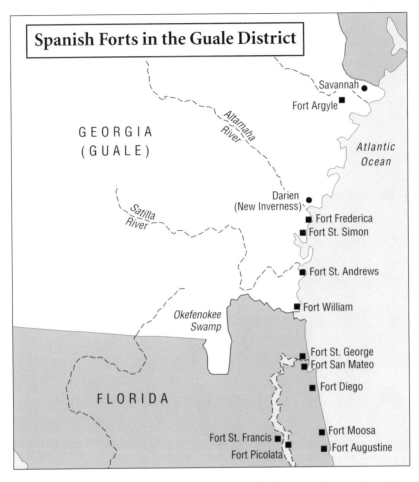

Spanish Forts in the Guale District

commerce in Guale that could compete with the growing trade of the English colonies to the north. With no potential economic gain in sight, Spanish authorities began to lose interest in Guale.

Their disenchantment grew with increasing attacks on the forts and missions by the Creeks and other Native Americans. The French and English provided the natives with weapons and other trade goods in exchange for raiding the Spanish establishments. To the west, along the Mississippi, the French built strong trade alliances with the Creek. The Creek were drawn to them because the French did not try to convert them to Christianity and tended to accept native ways of life. Moreover, after the colony of South Carolina was established in 1670, the English were also active in building trade alliances with the Creek, Cherokee, and some of the smaller coastal tribes.

The French and English built these trade alliances because they wanted the natives to drive the Spanish out of Guale, leaving the territory open to trade and settlement by others. This was not a joint effort between the French and English, however. The French wanted Guale so they could expand their growing trade empire east from the Mississippi to the Atlantic coast. For their part, the English were less interested in settling Guale than in ensuring that Spanish inhabitants would not invade the new colony of South Carolina or any of the other English colonies to the north. Removing the Spanish from Guale would lessen the chances of such an invasion.

By the 1680s it seemed that the French and English would be successful in forcing the Spanish out of Guale. During this decade the attacks by Creek and Cherokee tribes became so frequent that many Spaniards living at the missions and forts perished. Spanish authorities believed they did not possess enough troops to defend Guale, so the survivors fled to the main Spanish garrison at St. Augustine in Florida.

Although the Spanish abandoned their missions and forts, they had no intention of giving up their claims to the region, so the violence and struggle for control in Guale continued. Like the French and English, the Spanish managed to develop alliances with natives (mostly in the southeastern part of Guale), exchanging trade commodities for loyalty to Spain's interests. As a result, wars developed between tribes that had different European loyalties, and small parties of English, French, or Spanish traders were always subject to the threat of attack by natives. In 1704 the English decided to attack the Apalachees, who were allied with the Spanish. The commander, Colonel James Moore, recounted the attack in a letter to the South Carolina governor:

> We have totally destroyed all the people of four towns, so that we have left the Apalatchia [Apalachee] but that one town . . . [where] the people . . . run away altogether: their town, church, and fort, we burnt. . . . Apalatchia is now reduced to so feeble and low a condition, that it can neither support St. Augustine with provisions, nor distrust, endamage or frighten us. . . . In short, we have made Carolina as safe as the conquest of Apalatchia can make it.[5]

Despite the destruction of the Apalachee, the Spanish continued to incite raids on the English and French by forming alliances with other tribes. This state of restlessness and violence continued in Guale from the 1680s to about 1710.

In the early 1700s many Native Americans began to see the encroaching settlements of South Carolina as a greater threat than either other tribes or the French or Spanish, who did not have settlements sprouting up in native lands at the astounding rate the English did. The Creeks in particular grew uneasy as the Carolina settlements neared the Savannah River (the Georgia–South Carolina border today). The Creeks were repeatedly cheated out of their land, crops, and other goods by the English in South Carolina. Believing the English to be untrustworthy, the Creeks concluded that the only way to protect themselves and their lands was to drive the newcomers from the Carolina settlements.

Tensions mounted between the English and the Creek until 1715, when violence erupted in what became known as the Yamasee War (the Yamasee was just one tribe of the Creek confederacy, but many Creek tribes participated). That year a *micco* known to the English as

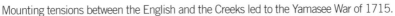

Mounting tensions between the English and the Creeks led to the Yamasee War of 1715.

Emperor Brim organized a massive force of native war parties with the intention of wiping out English settlements in South Carolina. Scores of settlers died in the ensuing massacres. Brim, a clever leader who successfully played the various European and Indian factions against each other to the benefit of the Creek, once sarcastically commented on English trustworthiness: "I never was Down to see your great King Yet I am as Streight [straight] hearted as the Best of them that has been Down; for I do not find that the Talk your great King gives them Lastes [lasts] any Longer than the present he makes them. As soon as the Present is wore out the Talk is forgotten."[6]

Just when it seemed that Brim and the Creeks would succeed in driving out the English, the tide turned against the natives. As the Yamasee force advanced toward Charles Town (present-day Charleston, South Carolina), the English townspeople organized a resistance party to repel the natives. Colonist Francis Yonge recounted the defense of Charles Town in a letter to England:

> In this war near 400 of the inhabitants were destroyed, with many houses and slaves, and great numbers of cattle, especially to the southward near Port Royal, from whence the inhabitants were entirely driven, and forced into the settlements near Charles-Town. This town [Charles Town] being fortified, they there had time to think what to do; and not mustering above 1200 men, they sent to Virginia and the neighboring colonies for assistance....[7]

Although outnumbered, the united colonists drove the natives back from Charles Town. Emperor Brim and his force retreated into the wilderness in Guale, beaten but not subdued.

In spite of their success at repelling the Creek, the South Carolina colonists feared further attacks by Native Americans. The settlers requested help from England to protect the colony. They wanted England to send soldiers to occupy Guale in order to prevent further Creek invasions. The Carolinians also were concerned about competition from other European peoples in North America, as historian Kenneth Coleman explains:

Pirates on the Georgia Coast

The crooked waterways and snug harbors of the Georgia coast offered good hiding places for French and English pirates who ambushed Spanish galleons (ships) loaded with treasure. The Spanish regularly carried gold and other valuable cargo from Mexico and South America back to Spain. Once a galleon was captured, the pirates looted the ship, imprisoned or—if a battle ensued—killed the crew, and headed home to England or France with the treasure.

In the early 1700s England was at war with Spain and hired privateers to raid the Spanish galleons. The war ended in 1713, but many of these privateers continued their raids without government authority.

One of the most famous English pirates to attack the region was Edward Thatch (sometimes also called Teach), otherwise known as Blackbeard. Blackbeard got his name from the long black beard he wore braided and tied with ribbons. He was known for blasting ships with forty cannon, disabling them, and then storming aboard loaded with pistols and knives in his belt, sword in hand, and a dagger in his teeth. Moreover, he sometimes tied small pieces of burning rope to his beard and hair, making him appear like a fearsome beast from hell.

Many legends developed about Blackbeard. Some claim that much of his pirate treasure is buried on Blackbeard Island off the coast of Georgia. Perhaps the most famous legend is the one that claims his headless ghost—Blackbeard was killed and decapitated in a fight off the North Carolina coast in 1718—still guards this treasure on Blackbeard Island.

Edward Thatch, known as Blackbeard, ambushed Spanish galleons from Georgia's harbors and waterways.

Beginning about 1700 the race between France, England, and Spain for control of the northern coast of the Gulf of Mexico increased the concern of Carolinians for their security. As the English secured no territory on the Gulf of Mexico, their entry would have to be through the land south of the Savannah River. It was fear of Spanish or French control of this territory that excited Carolinians. . . . [8]

The request fell on deaf ears, however, since England was then caught up in the problems of high unemployment and a poor economy. It continued to be ignored until fifteen years later when a forward-thinking member of Parliament used the South Carolina plea for help as a tool for establishing a "noble experiment" in the land called Guale. This experiment would be manifested as the founding of the colony of Georgia.

Chapter Two

Establishing the Colony: A Noble Experiment

For a long time, English colonists in North America were more interested than the English government itself in possessing Guale. However, the English Crown became an active participant in the struggle to dominate Guale in the 1730s. This newfound interest was spurred by the ideas of James Edward Oglethorpe, a respected member of Parliament who had great interest in humanitarian affairs.

More than any other person, Oglethorpe was responsible for the eventual English domination of the Guale region. He is considered by many historians to be the "Father of Georgia" because of his dedication to Georgia's people. Oglethorpe began this dedication by persuading the Crown to focus on the idea of starting a new colony as an answer to some of England's domestic problems.

Debtor Prisons and the Seed of an Idea

In the early 1700s the English government did not know how to solve the problem of the country's high unemployment. Towns were filled with beggars who wandered from place to place in a desperate search

James Edward Oglethorpe is known as the "Father of Georgia" because of his dedication to Georgia's people.

for work. Many could not pay their debts, and these people, called debtors, were thrown into prison.

English debtor prisons were horrible places. They were filthy and crowded, and prisoners frequently died from infectious diseases such as smallpox. James Oglethorpe's friend Robert Castell, an architect, was one of these debtors who ended up in prison. Castell was eventually forced to live in a cell with prisoners who had smallpox. He contracted the disease and subsequently died of it. When Oglethorpe learned of the circumstances of his friend's death, he was horrified. He was also determined to do something about the situation.

Oglethorpe requested that Parliament authorize a committee to investigate the conditions in debtor prisons. During the investigation, as chairperson of the committee, Oglethorpe personally visited many debtor prisons and collected evidence, including interviews with prisoners and recordings of his own observations. On several occasions he also brought along other members of the investigative committee—who normally only reviewed the chairperson's reports and made recommendations based on them—on his visits. Oglethorpe's first report to Parliament included a description of conditions at Fleet Prison, in which a Portuguese prisoner, Jacob Mendes Solas, was imprisoned:

> This Place is a Vault like those in which the Dead are Interr'd.
> . . . It [the cell] has no Chimney nor Fire-place, nor any Light
> but what comes over the Door, or through a Hole. . . . What

adds to the Dampness and Stench of the Place is, its being built over the Common-Shore and adjoining to the Sink and Dunghil[l] where all of the Nastiness of the Prison is cast. In this miserable Place the poor Wretch [Solas] was kept by . . . Bambridge [a notorious prison warden], Manacled and Shackled for near Two Months.[9]

This initial report led to further investigations of prisons all over England, which resulted in the development of reform laws for debtor prisons, beginning with the Debtors Act of 1730 passed unanimously by Parliament.

In spite of the success of the Debtors Act, Oglethorpe knew that improving prison conditions was not the answer to England's immense unemployment problem. A forward-looking and broad-minded person for his time, Oglethorpe developed an idea to help solve the problem.

Oglethorpe's first report to Parliament included a description of the horrible conditions at Fleet Prison (shown).

The Horrors of English Debtor Prisons

Several of the most horrible tortures that Oglethorpe discovered being inflicted in debtor prisons were described in his "Report Relating to Marshalsea Prison." In this excerpt, taken from his report in The Publications of James Edward Oglethorpe, *Oglethorpe recounts how two prisoners were treated, one for allegedly trying to escape, the other for unknown reasons:*

"In Order to extort from him a Confession of the Names of those, who had assisted him and others in their Attempt to escape, had screwed certain Instruments of Iron upon his Thumbs so close, that they had forced the Blood out of them, with exquisite Pain; after this he was carried into the Strong Room, where besides the other Irons which he had on, they fixed on his Neck and Hands an Iron Instrument, called a Collar, (like a pair of Tongs)....When they screwed the said Instrument close, his Eyes were ready to start out of his Head, the Blood gushed out of his Ears and Nose, he foamed at the Mouth, the Slaber [slobber] run down, and he made several Motions to speak, but could not; after these Tortures, he was confined in the Strong Room for many Days with a very heavy pair of Irons, called Sheers, on his Legs.

[The prison magistrates also] have made a Practice of Locking up Debtors, who displeased them, in the Yard with Humane Carcasses. One particular Instance of this Sort of Inhumanity was, of a Person whom the Keepers confined in that Part of the lower Yard which was then separated from the rest, whilst there were there two dead Bodies which had lain there Four Days; yet was He kept there with them Six Days longer, in which Time the Vermin devoured the Flesh from the Faces, eat the Eyes out of the Heads of the Carcasses, which were bloated, putrifyed, and turned green, during the poor Debtor's dismal Confinement with them."

The Georgia Charter

In 1730 Oglethorpe proposed to Parliament that England grant a charter to establish a new colony in the land the Spanish called Guale. He knew that colonists in South Carolina had been clamoring for a military presence in the region to protect the colony from Spanish invasion and attacks by Native Americans. Oglethorpe believed he could use this request as a tool to get the charter, with which he intended to build an ideal society in America—a place where honest, hardworking people whose only crime was that they could not pay their debts could get a fresh start.

Parliament, however, was not convinced, compelling Oglethorpe and the twenty supporters of his scheme to send a petition for the charter straight to King George II. The petition promised immense advantages to England by settling Guale. Not only would South Carolina be protected, but England could be relieved of many of its poor and unemployed. In addition, the new colony—to be named Georgia, after the king—would provide valuable new resources and commerce to the English empire. In June 1732 King George II granted the charter for the colony of Georgia, which stated its primary missions:

> Whereas we are Credibly Informed that many of our Poor Subjects are through misfortunes and want of Employment reduced to great necessities insomuch as by their labor they are not able to provide a maintenance for themselves and Families and if they had means to defray the Charge of Passage and other Expenses incident to new Settlements they would be glad to be settled in any of our new Provinces in America. . . .
>
> [W]hereby they might not only gain a Comfortable Subsistence for themselves and families but also Strengthen our Colonies and Encrease [increase] the trade Navigation and wealth of our realms and Whereas our Provinces in North America have been frequently Ravaged by Indian Enemies more especially that of South Carolina which in the late war . . . was laid waste

King George II granted the charter for the colony of Georgia in June 1732.

with Fire and Sword.... [W]hereas we think it highly becoming
Our Crown ... protect all our Loving Subjects....[10]

The new charter appointed Oglethorpe and his supporters as trustees
of the new colony, meaning that they were entrusted with the
management of Georgia. The trustees, who could not own land, hold
office, or receive a salary in Georgia, would be responsible for governing
the colony for twenty-one years, at which time the government would
be reestablished with a royal governor and legislative body similar to
those in the other colonies.

Preparing for the Journey

The trustees' first task was raising funds to finance the journey to
America and buy supplies needed to get started after arrival.
Parliament approved several appropriations to help establish the new
colony, which added up to $160,000 within the first two years. The
Bank of England also contributed a large amount of money for the
venture. The "noble experiment," as Georgia had become known,
quickly became a popular charity project for people all over England,
with several wealthy individuals and prosperous merchants donating
money and supplies.

As the trustees built up their store of supplies and funds, they also
went about selecting Georgia's first colonists. Although hundreds
applied, the trustees were very selective about whom they chose. While
Oglethorpe had envisioned a colony for the "worthy poor," the Crown
made it clear that it wanted a good number of settlers to be soldier-
colonists who would provide the military protection that was one of
the colony's primary goals. Nevertheless, many "charity colonists"—
whose way was paid by the trustees—were chosen to make the
journey. Before being selected, charity colonists were carefully
screened to ensure they "were in decayed Circumstances, and thereby
disabled from following any Business in England; and who, if in Debt,
had Leave from their Creditors to go, and such as were recommended
by the Minister ... of their respective Parishes."[11] These people were
not necessarily debtors, however. Many of those selected for the
journey were artisans or small tradesmen whose services would be
valuable in the new colony.

A Journey across the Atlantic

Peter Gordon was one of the passengers on board the Ann *in 1732 when Oglethorpe accompanied the first colonists from England to Georgia. This excerpt is from his recounting of the founding of Georgia,* The Journal of Peter Gordon, *and provides a picture of some of the dangers of the journey and also illustrates the benevolence Oglethorpe had for these colonists.*

"[After a child's christening ceremony] Mr. Oglethorpe ordered five gallons of brandy ... which being equally divided was three quarts to each mess [group of people who eat together] which consisted of five people, and to each mess was allowed half a fowl, with bacon, and greens, which was a very agreeable refreshment, our people having never been used to salt provissions before. The evening was spent, with mirth, and order and success to the intended Collony, and the Trustees. Healths went round chearfully [cheerfully].

The 26th about six in the morning Mr. Canons child about eight months old was found dead in the bed, and the same day about five oclock the child was putt in a wooden box, and buried in the sea, Doctor Herbert performing the prayers proper for the occasion. [As one of the appointed constables] Our principle bussiness on board was to see that in the serving out of the provissions and other refreshments, (which was done every day), each family, or mess, hade justice done them, and likewise that they should come regularly, and in their turns, to be serv'd and take particular care that no cursing, swearing, or any other indecency's should be comitted. And to prevent the danger of fire ... Mr. Kilbery was appoynted Corporall, and to see that all the candles between decks were putt out ever'y night at eight oclock. And in case that any of the passengers should be suddenly taken ill, a watch was appoynted, of our own young men, who took it in their turns ever'y night to attend in the steerage with a lanthorne [lantern] and candles."

Finally, on November 6, 1732, about 120 colonists (historical records disagree on the exact number) set sail on the *Ann* from Gravesend, England. On board ship, acting as the trustees' agent, was

Oglethorpe, who had volunteered to accompany the colonists to Georgia and act as unofficial leader.

Establishing Savannah

After two months crossing the Atlantic Ocean, the *Ann* reached the South Carolina coast, where colonist Peter Gordon wrote in his journal: "Jan: [the] 13th about nine in the morning we see two sails of shipps, and soon after we made [saw] land and stood for it, which we discovered in a short time to be Charles Town."[12] They did not land at Charles Town, but continued south to the Port Royal fort near the town of Beaufort.

While the colonists entertained themselves in Beaufort, Oglethorpe, accompanied by Colonel William Bull of South Carolina, continued up the Savannah River in search of a site to erect a town. Only eighteen miles inland he found a suitable site, located high on a bluff, which he described in a letter to the trustees in England:

> The river here forms a half-moon, along the south side of which the banks are about 40 feet high, and on the top a flat, which they call a bluff. The plain high ground extends into the country about 5 or 6 miles, and along the river about a mile. Ships that draw 12 feet of water can ride within ten yards of the bank.... The river is pretty wide, the water fresh, and ... you see its whole course to the sea ... and the other way you can see the River for about six miles up into the Country.[13]

Although Oglethorpe was impressed with the site, he was also determined to develop good relations with the local natives and he would not settle there if they objected. In his characteristic fair-mindedness, Oglethorpe went to the *micco* of the nearby Yamacraw tribe and asked permission to build a town on the bluff. He managed to persuade the elderly *micco*, Tomo-chi-chi, that the colonists were friendly, and obtained the permission.

Oglethorpe then returned to Beaufort and led the colonists toward Yamacraw Bluff, as he called the site. They arrived on February 12,

1733, and immediately set up tents and unloaded their supplies and belongings. The Yamacraw Indians, led by Tomo-chi-chi, came to greet the new settlers, as colonist Thomas Causton described in a letter home to England:

> Before them [the Indians] came a man dancing in antick [wild and strange] postures with a spread of white feathers in each hand as a token of friendship. . . . Then the King [Tomo-chi-chi] and all the men came in a regular manner and shook him by the hand. After that the Queen came and all the women did the like. Then Mr. Oglethorpe conducted them to his tent and made them sit down. [14]

Oglethorpe negotiated with Chief Tomo-chi-chi of the Yamacraw tribe for permission to build a colony on Yamacraw Bluff.

The Yamacraw people proved to be a great help to the colonists in the coming year, providing them with supplies of venison, turkey, and other fresh game when the colonists were too busy building to hunt.

The colonists were immediately put to work constructing buildings, using a layout that Oglethorpe and Colonel Bull had organized earlier for the new town, Savannah. One of the first buildings erected was a guardhouse, where a lookout and guns were kept. The streets were laid out at right angles, and public squares and meetinghouses were built. The construction of Savannah progressed so quickly that by March 23 three houses were completed and three more begun. Soon a courthouse, mill, well, church, and public stores building were finished.

Oglethorpe oversaw the construction and acted as a guide and model of industriousness for the colonists. He was arbitrator in all disputes, visited the sick, served on guard duty, and worked alongside the settlers in the backbreaking labor of erecting buildings and digging foundations for houses and streets. Although Oglethorpe was a strict taskmaster, the colonists became very fond of him, as reflected in a description of Savannah's progress by a South Carolina visitor: "He is extremely well beloved by all his People; the general title they give him is Father.... There are no idlers there; even the boys and girls do their part.... In short he has done a vast deal of work for the time...."[15]

The town of Savannah as it looked in the 1740s.

Regulations Under the Trustees

For a time Oglethorpe's sway with the colonists made it easy to enforce the strict rules and regulations of the new colony. Before the colonists had even left England, Oglethorpe and the other trustees had laid out the laws that would govern Georgia. For the most part these laws were designed to promote an ideal society—one where people would have fair opportunities for success and where everyone would be treated with equal respect. To this end, slavery was prohibited in Georgia. The trustees also disallowed slavery because they wanted the colonists to learn the moral lessons of thrift and industry by working their own land with their own two hands. Rum was also prohibited, primarily because it had been used by people in other colonies to steal land from intoxicated Indians. In fact, Georgia colonists could not trade with the natives at all unless they obtained a special permit from the trustees.

There were also limitations on land ownership. Charity colonists received a grant of fifty acres, while those who had paid their own way to America could own up to five hundred acres. Regardless of the property's size, all colonists were required to cultivate the land for at least three years and received seeds and tools from the trustees to accomplish this. The primary reason the trustees limited property size was to prevent the development of large plantations, which could, in turn, lead to the growth of a ruling aristocratic class. The trustees did not want an aristocracy in Georgia because it would put the ruling power in the hands of a wealthy few, a situation inconsistent with their ideal of an egalitarian society.

The Colonists Complain

Despite the hard work of the colonists, the opportunities for advancement there, and Oglethorpe's strict guidance, the colony of Georgia did not thrive during its first two decades for several reasons. One was that after the initial three-year period was over, some of the original colonists left Georgia when they saw South Carolinians just across the Savannah River growing rich on their large plantations run with slave labor. The Georgia colonists began to resent the prohibition of slavery in their colony and wanted to reap the same financial rewards as the South Carolinians.

Slaves work a field in South Carolina. Property limitations and the prohibition of slavery made Georgia unattractive to potential settlers.

The colonists were also unhappy with the property regulations. They wanted to be able to expand their properties and develop them into large plantations. Many also thought the rules regarding inheritance were unfair, as colonist Peter Gordon wrote in his journal:

> That their lands were lyable [liable] to severall forfeitures, and that in case of dying without male issue [sons] their lands were to revert to the Trustees. This gave occasion, to one of the people [to inform] the Trustees, that as he hade [had] only . . . a daughter he could by no means think of going . . . alledging that his daughter being equally dear to him as a sone [son], he could never enjoy any peace of mind, for the apprehension [fear] of dying there, and leaving his child, destitute and unprovided for, not having a right to inherit or posses any part of his reall estate. . . . [16]

Property limitations and the prohibition of slavery made Georgia very unattractive to many potential settlers. To Oglethorpe's disappointment, England's poor and oppressed did not flock in droves to settle the new colony. The people who came to the southern part of America in the mid-1700s were primarily seeking better economic opportunities. They would go where they had the greatest opportunity to build wealth—which at the time was South Carolina rather than Georgia. In all, only about two thousand charity colonists ever came to Georgia.

Another reason new settlers did not come to Georgia was because of the threat of Spanish invasion. Although the Spanish had been driven out of the region in the 1680s, Spain had not relinquished its claim to the territory. Soon after the English began to colonize Georgia, Spain realized that it had to act quickly in order to protect this claim. Spanish spies were sent into Savannah to assess English intentions.

The Spanish Threat

Rumors of Spanish spies compelled Oglethorpe to return to England in 1734 to seek military aid. He persuaded Parliament to appropriate funds for the building of a new town, with an adjacent military fort, on St. Simons Island off the Georgia coast. In addition, he recruited soldier-settlers to populate the new town and defend the fort. Oglethorpe arrived at St. Simons in early 1736 and founded the town of Frederica, and the nearby fort became the major military stronghold of the colony.

Spies reported the construction of the new English fortification to Spanish authorities in Florida. In retaliation the Spanish tried to

In 1736 Oglethorpe founded the town of Frederica on St. Simons Island near Fort Frederica (shown below).

weaken the colony by seizing and searching British merchant ships off the coast of Florida and Georgia. Moreover, Indians loyal to the Spanish increased their raids on English towns along the Savannah River.

As the threat of Spanish invasion grew, Oglethorpe realized that Georgia needed still more protection. He again traveled to England in 1737, where Parliament gave him more funds to finance military operations in Georgia. It also permitted him to raise a regiment of soldiers for Georgia's defense, naming him commander in chief of all British troops in Georgia and South Carolina. The following year Oglethorpe returned to Georgia and promptly stationed six hundred regular troops at the St. Simons fort.

In the meantime, a shipmaster named Robert Jenkins had sparked a public furor when he reported to Parliament that the Spanish had cut off one of his ears when they captured him and his ship smuggling goods in Spanish waters. The story enraged the English people, compelling Parliament to authorize Oglethorpe to officially make war on the Spanish in 1739.

War with Spain

In response, Oglethorpe added recruits from Georgia and South Carolina and Indian allies to the regular troops at St. Simons, mobilizing an army of about two thousand men. In 1740 he led the British troops south, capturing Spanish forts, until they arrived at St. Augustine where they lay siege to the fort and nearby town. However, the siege was abandoned after thirty-eight days because the British force had been weakened by disease and growing discontent among the men. Oglethorpe then withdrew to St. Simons.

For the next two years skirmishes continued between English and Spanish soldiers in Georgia. The Spanish continued to capture British ships, cutting Georgia off from news and supplies from England and severely damaging the colony's trade. The Spanish continually attacked coastal settlements while Indians loyal to Spain subjected the inland towns to raids. So many men were away from their homes defending the colony that the towns were left almost defenseless.

By the spring of 1742 the situation for the English in Georgia was growing ever more dire. England had become too distracted by

At the Battle of Bloody Marsh Oglethorpe defeated a much larger Spanish force and ended Spanish influence in Georgia.

problems at home to keep sending troops and supplies to Georgia. Oglethorpe's army was down to about nine hundred men, more than half of whom were Indian allies. That year Oglethorpe learned that a Spanish invasion fleet was on its way toward Frederica with three thousand soldiers who were under orders to destroy the forts and towns of Georgia and South Carolina.

Despite being grossly outnumbered, Oglethorpe refused to give up the fight. Although the Spanish force easily captured the St. Simons fort, Oglethorpe moved his troops to nearby Frederica. They harassed the Spanish soldiers until the next morning, when a company of two hundred Spanish men attempted to take Frederica. The British soldiers (a division of mostly Highlander Scots) managed to repel them, but later that day another larger company of Spanish soldiers marched on the town. This time Oglethorpe's men could not hold Frederica and they retreated along the road between the fort and the town.

Along the way, the British troops were struck with an idea—they decided to hide in the thick surrounding woods and wait to ambush the pursuing Spanish. In a stroke of luck for Oglethorpe's men, the Spanish troops stopped at the place along the road where they were hidden. Assuming that the British were gone, they stacked their guns and began to prepare supper. It was then that the British force launched its attack, killing all but a few of the three hundred Spaniards. This decisive event became known as the Battle of Bloody Marsh because those present claimed that a nearby marsh ran with the blood of the dead and wounded.

The Battle of Bloody Marsh might not have ended the Spanish offensive but for another decision made in poor judgment by the Spanish just a few days later. Disillusioned by their defeat at Bloody Marsh, the Spanish military authorities mistook a fleet of South Carolinian commercial vessels for British military reinforcements. Convinced they would soon be defeated, the Spanish force abandoned the fort on St. Simons and retreated to Florida.

In spite of the military victory and its clearing the way for unimpeded further settlement by the English, Oglethorpe was not to enjoy the fruits of his labor in Georgia. Within a few years after the end of the War of Jenkins' Ear, as the Spanish invasion had come to be called, the ideal society he had so carefully constructed yielded to the demands of the Georgian people. The resulting changes in Georgia would lead to a significant flux in the daily lives of its colonists.

Chapter Three

Changes in Daily Life in Colonial Georgia

S ince the main reasons the English Parliament supported development of the Georgia colony were its potential economic wealth and its importance as a military stronghold, it was predictable that Oglethorpe's noble ideal of egalitarian lifestyles for all would eventually have to give way. The strict regulations on slavery, property ownership, and Indian trade were not conducive to developing an economy as prosperous as South Carolina's. As a result, people did not want to live in Georgia, and the population failed to grow. In fact, during the Spanish invasion, colonists had fled Georgia's towns in fearful droves, many of them going north to the Carolinas and Virginia, where they began to thrive.

For these reasons, Parliament became dissatisfied with the trustees' management of the colony by the mid-1740s. Georgia had not met its expectations in contributing to the wealth of the British Empire. The British Crown pressured the trustees to make concessions to the colonists' demands. These concessions and the subsequent authority

Despite their fondness for Oglethorpe (pictured), Georgia colonists grew increasingly dissatisfied with the lack of economic prosperity in Georgia.

of a royal colonial government brought major changes in the daily lives of Georgia's colonists.

End of Trustee Authority

Under the management of the trustees, the colonists of Georgia did not participate in the government of their colony. The original charter issued in 1732 made no mention of a representative (elected) assembly. The trustees believed that the first colonists of Georgia did not possess self-governing skills. These skills could be acquired only over time and through experience with self-sufficiency and independence on the Georgia frontier.

The regulations of the colony had been set by the trustees prior to its founding. The trustees expected the regulations to be followed until the charter was due to be relinquished after twenty-one years. Thus there was no way for colonists to change the rules they did not like, such as the prohibition of slavery. Although the colonists complained about many regulations, the management of the trustees was generally fair and just, and Oglethorpe, as unofficial leader, made decisions with the benefit of all Georgians in mind. Never once did he abuse the authority he had been given, and this commanded great respect from many colonists.

Despite their fondness for Oglethorpe, however, the colonists grew increasingly dissatisfied with the lack of economic prosperity in Georgia, which they viewed as a direct result of the colony's ban on slavery. Their complaints reached Parliament and the king, and both refused requests from the trustees for more funding after 1743. One such complaint was addressed to the trustees:

We . . . unanimously join to lay before you, with the utmost Regret, the following Particulars. . . . Timber is the only thing we have here which we might export . . . yet we cannot manufacture it for a foreign market but at double the Expence of other Colonies; as for Instance . . . with the Allowance of Negroes [in South Carolina], load Vessels with that Commodity at One half the Price that we can do. . . . It is very well known, that Carolina can raise everything that this Colony can; and they having their Labour so much cheaper, will always ruin our Market, unless we are in some measure on a Footing with them. . . . [you] are not insensible of the Numbers that have left this Province, not being able to support themselves and Families any longer. . . .[17]

The British government felt that it had amply supported the development of Georgia, and now it was time for the colony to prove its worth. However, they found it sorely lacking and refused further requests for aid. Without financial support from England the trustees could no longer manage the colony. Gradually they were forced to make concessions to the colonists' demands.

At this juncture Oglethorpe left the colony, never to return after 1743. He was present at the first trustee meetings in England that changed the rules, but after 1749 he abandoned the meetings, refusing to participate in the dismantling of his "noble experiment." Eventually both the restrictions on property ownership and rum were lifted.

It was the legalization of slavery in 1749, however, which most galled Oglethorpe. Allowing slavery in Georgia signaled the end of his dream of creating an egalitarian society. Now Georgia would be no different from the other southern colonies. The other trustees were also disillusioned with the colony and in 1751 gave up the charter to Parliament, two years before it was due.

The legalization of slavery in Georgia in 1749 ended Oglethorpe's dream of creating an egalitarian society.

Government Under the Royal Charter

The following year, in June 1752, a new charter was issued and Georgia officially became a royal colony with a system of government like that of the other English royal colonies in America. Under the new charter Georgia was divided into "parishes," which were religious and legislative districts. These parishes had no local government body and functioned simply as administrative units. Each parish elected representatives to the Commons House of Assembly which met in Savannah. Voting rights were allowed to men who owned at least fifty acres of land. Only male colonists who owned at least five hundred acres of land were eligible to serve in the Commons House, which included about twenty members.

The new charter also provided for an Upper House, whose members were responsible for aiding and advising the governor. The Upper House members were not elected. Rather, they were appointed by the king upon the advice of the governor.

The governor held the real authority in Georgia's colonial government. He was both the civil and military ruler, appointed by the king. The governor could appoint political and military officers, preside over courts, control land grants, and veto any bill passed by the assembly. He also had the power to convene, adjourn, or dissolve the assembly.

Georgia's first royal governor, John Reynolds, was very unpopular with the colonists because of his dictatorial style. He consistently refused to cooperate with the Commons House and disregarded the needs of the people. Eventually the Commons House petitioned the king to address the colonists' complaints about Reynolds. The king, who wanted someone who could restore harmony and bring prosperity to Georgia, removed Reynolds from office.

From that point on the governors of colonial Georgia enjoyed a good deal of popularity with the people. Under the guidance of wise and cooperative governors the assembly developed into an effective lawmaking body. Great strides were made in the commerce, wealth, and population growth of the colony, and finally Georgia began to prosper economically.

Economic Changes

The legalization of slavery attracted many newcomers to Georgia in the 1750s. Gradually the population increased and the economy began to flourish. However, it was the end of the French and Indian War in 1763 that brought renewed energy to Georgia's economic boom. At this time Spain ceded Florida to England, removing the threat of Spanish invasion in Georgia. In addition, the French vacated the Mississippi River Valley in the west. The Indians were left with no allies in the French or the Spanish, thus forcing them to get along with their English neighbors. This resulted in their ceding new land in the southwest part of the colony to Georgia in 1763 and 1773.

With the ban on slavery and the threat of foreign invasion removed, and the opening of new lands for settlement, people flocked to Georgia from the Carolinas and Virginia. Between 1750 and 1773 the population grew from 5,000 to 33,000, nearly half of whom were slaves. Most people who migrated to Georgia after 1750 were in pursuit of greater economic wealth, and they saw slavery as necessary to this pursuit, as historian Kenneth Coleman explains:

> Advocates of slavery argued that whites could not do hard work in a climate such as Georgia's and that the prohibition of slavery prevented the colony from achieving its full development. They ... cited as proof that rice production in South Carolina was carried on entirely by slaves. They argued that Negroes were cheaper to acquire and to maintain than were white servants. Certainly Carolinians raised more with slave labor than was raised in Georgia with free or servant labor.[18]

Before the legalization of slavery, most colonists grew small crops of corn, rice, peas, potatoes, and pumpkins using their own labor and sometimes the help of white servants. However, the early colonists were not used to the backbreaking work of farming on the frontier. Many of them had been townspeople and thought they were above doing manual labor. In addition, crop yields were often unproductive and did not reap enough surplus to pay for the servant labor or even farming tools. Part of the problem was that the colonists were inexperienced farmers and did not know proper methods for farming the sandy soil. In addition the long, hot, dry summers of the region were not suited for some of the crops the colonists tried to grow.

Despite these problems the colonists blamed their economic woes on the absence of a cheap labor force—slaves.

Although the legalization of slavery in Georgia did initiate economic growth, most people in Georgia remained farmers on small inland properties with few if any slaves. These farmers grew food staples (wheat, corn, potatoes), tobacco, and cotton, none of which was highly profitable.

The coastal plantations, often larger and more prosperous, produced rice and indigo. Their crops covered vast tracts of land worked by many slaves. Botanist William Bartram visited Georgia in 1773 and described rice cultivation there in his writings:

> I viewed with pleasure this gentleman's [Bartram's host] . . . improvements in agriculture; particularly in the growth of rice, and in his machine for shelling that valuable grain, which stands in the water almost from the time it is sown, until within a few days before it is reaped, when they draw off the water by sluices, which ripens it all at once, and when the heads . . . are dry ripe, it is reaped and left standing in the field, in small ricks, until all the straw is quite dry, when it is hauled, and stacked in the barn yard. [19]

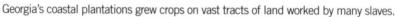

Georgia's coastal plantations grew crops on vast tracts of land worked by many slaves.

The Silk Industry in Georgia

Raw silk was a major trade commodity in Georgia for many years and had come to the colony in its first year. The trustees had dreamed of making Georgia's silk a major rival to European silk producers and had regularly ordered shipments of silkworm eggs sent to the colony. In fact, silk experts from Italy were hired during Georgia's early years to teach the colonists how to cultivate silkworms and reel (to unwind from the cocoon) quality silk. The silk was then sold to textile factories where it was woven into silk fabric. In the peak year of 1751, 496 pounds of raw silk were exported.

Silkworm raising was described in a 1732 article of the South Carolina Gazette:

"It becomes a pretty big worm and shuts itself up in its cod or ball it weaves itself. This looks like a greenish bean. At length it becomes a butterfly after making its passage from its silken sepulchre. . . . [However, the worm is prevented from leaving the cocoon and breaking the silk thread of sometimes six miles in length and they are] taken down and put in a moderate oven or exposed to the sun to kill the maggot. The cods [cocoons] are different colors, yellow, orange and flesh color. Some are green, some sulphur color, some white. . . . The worm itself can be fed to poultry."

Unfortunately, Georgia's climate did not agree with silkworms or the mulberry trees they survived on. Late frosts often killed the mulberry leaves on which the silkworms fed, and as a result many worms perished prior to the cocoon stage. In addition, the labor required to care for the worms and the cocoons, and to reel the silk, was costly. Silk production could not compete with other produce and it gradually declined in importance.

Most of these farmers sold their surplus rice to merchants who traded with the West Indies. Indigo was primarily exported to Britain for making the blue dye used in fabrics.

The trade merchants sold many commodities in addition to farm produce, usually through the Savannah port. They also sold surplus items obtained from shopkeepers and artisans. In the early years of the colony items such as bear oil, native herbs, lumber, wine, potash, and raw silk commonly appeared in the trade accounts. After 1760 rice and indigo became the major trade goods, and the commerce of the colony increased, as a 1773 letter written by Governor James Wright reveals:

> [To Great Britain] we export Deer skins, Rice, Indico [indigo], Naval stores [tar and pitch] and Sundry [various] other Articles. . . . To the West Indies we send Rice, Corn, Pease, Lumber, Shingles, Cattle, Horses and Live Stock also Barrelled Beef and Pork. . . . We have entered and cleared at the Custom house in the Port of Savannah for the last year one hundred and sixty one sails of Vessels of Different sorts and at Sunbury fifty six . . . there may be employed seventeen hundred seafaring men.[20]

Despite the rise of prosperity in the colony, the people did not apply their new wealth to improving many of the social institutions in Georgia, including education. Although literacy was valued, formal schooling took a backseat far behind the maintenance of economic success—which was, after all, the primary incentive that brought most colonists to Georgia in the first place.

Education in Colonial Georgia

The focus on economic success reduced the role of education in most Georgians' lives. Many parents believed it was more important for their children to learn the business of managing a successful plantation than it was for them to attend school.

Children who did attend school lived mostly in towns. Children who lived in the countryside often could not safely walk to schools several miles away because of danger from inclement weather, hostile Indians, or wild animals. Moreover, their help was often needed to work the farm. Nevertheless, Savannah ran a free public school during its early years, and all over the colony private schools sprang up, such as the one described in this 1774 *Georgia Gazette* advertisement:

Just opened, at the west end of the Commons . . . [a school] where he [unnamed teacher] teaches Latin, English, French, and other Languages, gramatically; Writing and Arithmetick, both vulgar and Decimal; and several other Liberal Arts and Sciences. . . . Book-Keeping after the Italian Method; and . . . the use of the Small Sword [fencing]. . . .[21]

Many of these schools were boarding schools for either boys or girls and offered curriculums similar to the one offered by the advertised school, and also navigation (the common term for commerce at the time), needlework, dancing, and music. These schools were attended only by children whose parents could afford the tuition, however.

In general, education for most children meant hands-on practical learning on the farm or in a shop. Many boys—often those who came after the firstborn son who was bound to inherit the farm—were apprenticed to artisans in the nearest town. These boys usually spent seven years, from the age of nine, living with and learning a trade from their "master" before going into business on their own as a cobbler, bricklayer, tailor, blacksmith, silversmith, or carpenter.

Girls from wealthy families were expected to learn skills in the arts and social etiquette. Frequently their studies included playing a

In the early years of the Georgia colony, education for most children meant hands-on practical learning on the farm or in a shop.

The Bethesda Orphanage and School

In 1740 the Reverend George Whitefield founded Bethesda in Savannah as an orphanage where children could receive formal training in both education and religion. He also founded it as an outlet for his Methodist views, which in Georgia, where there was no established church, he could express without harassment from the Anglican Church.

The children who lived at Bethesda, who were collected by Whitefield from all the colonies and England, adhered to a very strict, narrow schedule and set of rules. The purpose was to override sinful behaviors by fostering industriousness and piety in the children. They were up at five in the morning for prayers, then sang hymns at church, and ate breakfast at seven. From eight to ten they worked, usually at chores or crafts, and from ten to noon they had lessons, followed by lunch. They worked again until two, and then had lessons until four. Between four and six in the evening the children worked again, followed by supper. They attended church again at seven, and at eight the teachers questioned the children on religious topics, with the intent of making them aware of their sinfulness and the need to call upon God for help. They finally went to bed at ten.

Over time the school began to offer lessons to children outside the orphanage, and gradually Bethesda became a boarding school that was reputed to provide the best education in Georgia. The curriculum, which began simply with religion, artisanship skills, and basic reading, grammar,

musical instrument, singing, and dancing. However, many girls did learn some of the business of running a farm, often out of necessity. Women did not go on to college as higher education was considered unnecessary for being a wife and mother.

Higher education was a rare attainment even for boys in colonial Georgia. Only the sons of the most affluent coastal planters attended college, and most went to institutions in the north such as Harvard (in Massachusetts), Yale (in Connecticut), or William and Mary (in Virginia). The primary motivation for getting a college education was simply that book-learning was expected of gentlemen from the leading aristocratic families.

and arithmetic, evolved to include subjects such as the classics, higher mathematics, and languages.

When Whitefield died in 1770 he willed Bethesda to his friend Selina, countess of Huntingdon, with the hope that it would one day become a Methodist college. Today Bethesda still operates.

Founded in 1740 by the Reverend George Whitefield, the Bethesda Orphan Asylum provided formal training in education and religion.

Religion in Colonial Georgia

Religion was also secondary to commercial gain in the daily lives of Georgia colonists. Since it was not considered necessary for the pursuit of wealth, religion had not been a major force in the colony's development. Only a few people came to Georgia seeking religious freedom, and the colonists were from diverse faiths. From the beginning Georgia was one of the most liberal colonies in regard to religious tolerance, which was protected in the 1732 charter: "[T]here shall be liberty of conscience allowed in the Worship of God to all persons inhabiting . . . our said Province And that all persons Except Papists [Roman Catholics] shall have Free Exercise of their Religion. . . ."[22]

Since officially Georgia was an English colony, the Church of England (Anglican), became the established church during the royal government years. However, unlike the Puritans, who wielded considerable authority in New England, the Anglicans in Georgia did not base political power on religious affiliation. Anglicans would have faced a difficult challenge in controlling the government because of the diversity of creeds in Georgia. Plenty of other Protestant churches flourished in the towns of colonial Georgia, including Lutheran, Presbyterian, Methodist, Quaker, and Baptist.

Religious diversity also resulted in widely varying levels of church attendance among the colonists despite legislation that mandated a certain code of behavior on the Sabbath. By law, travel was forbidden on Sundays, and everyone had to attend church. Although many people did so, just as many ignored the Sabbath by merrymaking at the local taverns, hunting, or managing their farms. However, the religious laws were seldom enforced.

The Role of Immigrants in Colonial Georgia

To a large degree the religious diversity in Georgia was due to its equally diverse ethnic population. In the early days of Georgia's colonization, oppressed people from many parts of Europe came to the colony seeking a better life. Some of these immigrants sought economic opportunity while others—though a much smaller percentage of the population—wanted freedom from religious persecution. They came from all walks of life—missionaries, artisans, common laborers, even scientists. Others came as indentured servants, people who spent an agreed-upon term of service to another person in return for their passage to America. Often those who came for religious reasons proved to be the most industrious of the colonists. In 1734 the town of Ebenezer was settled by German-speaking Salzburgers from Austria who had been forced from their homeland by Catholic rulers. The hardworking group immediately started up a silkworm industry. They became the most successful farmers in Georgia during the trustee years of the colony, largely because they worked together on common plots of land instead of individual tracts. Moreover, the Salzburgers were not afraid of hard labor.

The Moravians from Bohemia were another religiously motivated group, who arrived in 1735 with the goal of educating the Indians and converting them to Christianity. They became unpopular with most other Georgians during the War of Jenkins' Ear because they refused to participate in military action. The Moravians were so harassed they were driven to migrate to Pennsylvania between 1738 and 1740.

Other religious groups who came to Georgia were not seeking religious freedom but rather economic opportunity. In 1768, Quakers arrived from North Carolina and quickly enlarged their town of Wrightsboro—although by the 1780s the town had been abandoned, largely in protest of the growth of slavery in the colony. Likewise, Puritan Congregationalists settled at Midway and became some of the most ardent supporters of independence during the Revolution.

Austrians from Salzburg land in Georgia. Oppressed peoples from many parts of Europe came to the colony seeking a better life.

During the first year of Georgia's settlement, a group of about forty Jews arrived in Savannah. Despite the protests of the trustees, Oglethorpe welcomed them. There was a doctor, Samuel Nunes, among them, who helped the many colonists who fell ill during that first summer in Savannah. Dr. Nunes's skills were highly valued, since the physician who had come to Georgia with the first settlers had died. The Jews became prominent citizens of Savannah, known for their generosity and goodwill.

Other ethnic groups came for purely economic reasons. The town of Highgate was settled by French-speaking Swiss. Many Irish, Welsh, Dutch, and German-speaking people came as indentured servants who, after their term of service, founded towns such as Acton and Vernonburg, where they labored hard on their own land.

In the south, Scottish Highlanders established the town of Darien in 1736 and became known as excellent planters and cattle raisers. They had been recruited by the trustees to settle near the southern border and serve as guardians against the Spanish because of the Highlanders' reputation as able defenders. Soon after their arrival they immediately constructed a battery of four cannons, a guardhouse, a chapel, and some huts. Darien gained a reputation for being "one of the settlements where the people have been most industrious. . . ."[23] The Highlanders were Presbyterians who spoke mostly Gaelic and wore traditional plaid tartans.

The diversity of the immigrants who settled Georgia contributed to civil and political conflict there during the Revolutionary era. Those with English backgrounds tended to be more loyal to the British government than those from other parts of Europe. In addition, the newness of the Georgia colony and its recent rise to self-government and increased prosperity led many Georgians to question whether they wanted to risk cutting their ties to the guidance and support of England. This unique perspective made Georgians reluctant to join the patriot cause of independence.

Chapter Four

The Revolution and Georgia's Civil War

Recent prosperity and political immaturity made Georgia slower than most other American colonies to respond to the spirit of protest and demand independence after England began to impose taxes on them. These factors, along with the presence of an ethnically and religiously diverse population, contributed to civil disagreement in Georgia—a disagreement that temporarily held the colony at a standstill, preventing it from making a commitment either for or against American independence in the early Revolutionary years.

Although Georgia did eventually join the patriot (pro-independence) cause, throughout the Revolutionary War its people were beset with political violence, not only between patriots and British loyalists but within the ranks of the patriots themselves. Despite this, Georgians sacrificed a great deal on the home front, as much of the colony was occupied by the British during the middle and later years of the war. Moreover, with its small frontier population and borders exposed to the British, Georgia was militarily weak.

Reaction to the Stamp Act

Following the end of the French and Indian War, England decided to tax its American colonies in order to pay its war debt. This angered many colonists because the taxes were passed by Parliament, a political body in which they had no voice. The colonists thought this was unfair since British subjects in England were represented by members of Parliament.

One of the first of these acts passed by Parliament was the Stamp Act in 1765, which required licenses, newspapers, and legal documents to bear a stamp that had to be purchased from the English government. Although Georgians were as incensed about the Stamp Act as most other American colonists, they were much slower to denounce the Crown and

Colonists burn Stamp Act papers in protest of the Stamp Act.

less violent in their reaction than people in other colonies. Because Georgia was still a new colony—only thirty years old—many of its colonists could still remember their time in England and identified very closely with the mother country. As a result they were more reluctant to turn their backs on England, even when they believed their rights were being usurped. In addition, Georgia was enjoying the

Governor James Wright, a highly effective and greatly respected leader who was influential in colonial politics.

greatest prosperity and wealth it had yet known, and many colonists did not want to jeopardize this new economic security.

Georgia was also slow to denounce the Stamp Act because its royal colonial leaders were very popular. Governor James Wright was a highly effective leader who had the best interests of Georgians at heart. He was greatly respected by most Georgians and highly influential in colonial politics. Wright was also an unswervingly loyal servant of the British king. He professed to be dedicated to both royal and Georgian interests, saying, "It has ever been my study to discharge my duty both to the King & People with integrity, & to the utmost of my power...."[24] Up to the time of the Stamp Act, Governor Wright had experienced almost no conflict with the Commons House in developing or enforcing legislation.

When England passed the Stamp Act, however, the atmosphere of tranquility began to disappear. Although the Commons House did not oppose the Stamp Act tax outright, it did oppose the manner in which the tax had been implemented—that is, without colonial representation in Parliament. Governor Wright took precautions to limit organized resistance to the act. When Massachusetts called for a Stamp Act Congress—a group of delegates from each colony that would decide how to deal with the Stamp Act—Wright would not convene a special assembly of the Commons House (it was not in session at the time), thus preventing the house from choosing and sending delegates to the congress.

Among the Georgia colonists, reactions to the Stamp Act were mixed. Much of the resistance was built up by Liberty Boys—a group of radical independent colonists associated with the Sons of Liberty of New England—from Charles Town in South Carolina, where public opposition to the act was strong. The Liberty Boys were responsible for a demonstration in October 1765, held on the anniversary of King George's ascension to the throne. During the usual public celebration a group of colonists carried an effigy of a stamp distributor through the streets of Savannah.

Early in 1766 the opposition became more volatile. In January, two hundred protesters marched on Savannah, intending to intimidate the governor into denouncing the Stamp Act. Wright, however, gathered fifty-six Rangers (Georgia royal soldiers) and managed to disperse the group, chastising them for showing disrespect to the king.

Although Wright had successfully headed off the opposition, he took measures to heavily guard the stamps. As a result Georgia was the only colony that actually sold any stamps when the Stamp Act took effect. Within a month, however, opposition had become so strong that Wright sent the rest of the stamps safely off on a vessel to England and allowed ships to leave Savannah's port with certificates stating that no stamps were available.

Once the Stamp Act was repealed in July 1766, Wright was relieved that the issue was resolved, and the colonists of Georgia celebrated what they thought was a victory over Parliament. It soon became clear to them that it was a short-lived victory at best, with the passage of the Townshend Acts that followed.

The Spirit of Opposition Grows

The Townshend Acts led to the first official action the Commons House took against the governor's authority. These four acts taxed items such as tea, paper, glass, and lead, and like the Stamp Act they were opposed because they had been implemented without colonial involvement or consent. In 1768 the Commons House formally petitioned the Crown for repeal of the Townshend Acts:

We acknowledge a constitutional subordination to the mother country and to its supreme legislature, as the same time, with inexpressible concern, we must lament, that by their [Parliament's] imposition of internal taxes [they usurp] our indubitable right [to grant] away our own property; and we are thereby prevented from a compliance with any requisition, which your Majesty may graciously please to make, and which, to the utmost of our abilities, we have hitherto always most cheerfully obeyed. [25]

In response to colonial opposition the acts were repealed, except for the tax on tea, in 1770. There followed a few years of peace, and resistance to the Crown fell to a low. Things might have remained peaceable in Georgia but for the actions of the Sons of Liberty in Boston, Massachusetts.

Rise of the Whig-Tory Division

Although the tax on tea remained, not many people in Georgia bothered to resist it. However, the radical element in the northern colonies, especially Massachusetts, was much stronger, and in 1774 the Sons of Liberty dumped tea in Boston port into the harbor to protest the tax. When, in response, Parliament passed the Boston Port Bill,

In 1774 the Sons of Liberty dumped tea into the Boston harbor to protest the tea tax.

which closed the harbor, and revoked the Massachusetts charter, furious opposition arose in the colonies, including Georgia. Some colonies, especially those in the north, began to talk about separating from England. Although not all the colonies supported independence at this time, most agreed that the colonies needed to act as a united front in order to resist England's actions. Therefore a meeting was called, and representatives—called delegates—were invited from each of the colonies. This meeting was the beginning of the Continental Congress.

Incensed Georgians called a meeting for July 1774 at Tondee's Tavern in Savannah to consider sending delegates to the intercolonial congress. Although no delegates were selected, participants at the meeting reconvened in August, where eight resolutions were passed denouncing the actions of the Crown:

> Resolved ... that his Majesty's subjects in America owe the same allegiance, and are entitled to the same rights, privileges, and immunities with their fellow-subjects in Great Britain ... that an act of Parliament ... for blockading the port and harbor of Boston is contrary to our idea of the British Constitution: ... that the act for abolishing the charter of Massachusetts Bay tends to the subversion of American rights ... the Parliament hath not, nor ever had, any right to tax his Majesty's American subjects ... That we will concur with our sister colonies in every constitutional measure to obtain redress of American grievances....[26]

Unfortunately for the colonists who attended the meeting and agreed to the resolutions, getting sister colonies to concur was going to be difficult due to controversy over the resolutions. In fact, seven petitions objecting to the resolutions were circulated in several parishes. Most objections related to a fear that in reprisal Britain would not send military support to guard colonists from Indian attacks, or that the resolutions should have been in the form of a petition rather than a challenge to royal authority.

Officially the Commons House, while it objected to the recent acts of Parliament, was not ready to formally oppose the Crown. Therefore,

Georgia did not immediately join the union of colonies at the First Continental Congress in 1774. Savannah was divided in its political leanings, and the "upcountry" (the inland region at higher elevations than coastal areas), whose residents generally supported independence, also included communities that were loyal to England. In many cases the older settlers were loyal while the newer settlers and the younger generation of the old wanted independence. Historian Spencer B. King explains the reasons for such divisions:

> Diversity of nationalities, economic interests, and religious affiliations were all factors in setting off many Georgians into either the camp of the Whigs [pro-independence] or the Tories [loyalists for England]. Opposition came from the up-country settlers, many of whom had never seen England. Drifting into the Georgia hills from Virginia and the Carolinas and even farther north, these settlers were truly American with a spirit of independence characteristic of the frontier. Yet Savannah had its freedom-loving patriots who resented the efforts of Parliament to shift to the colonies some of the burden of imperial debt incurred during the French and Indian War. These, in many instances, were the children of Tories. Thus, many families were divided in sentiment.[27]

Even after the other colonies had decided that independence was the only way to resolve problems with England, Georgia continued to balk at the idea, even its Whig leaders. St. John's Parish, settled mostly by former New Englanders, was so disgusted by Georgia's lack of commitment to colonial rights that it voted to secede from the Colony and asked to be allowed to join South Carolina. It also sent its own delegate, Lyman Hall, to the Continental Congress.

Georgia soon paid for its failure to join the patriot cause. First, South Carolina broke off trade relations with Georgia: "Resolved, that we will, from henceforth, have no Trade, Commerce, Dealings, or Intercourse with the said Colony of Georgia; but will hold them as unworthy of the rights of freemen, as inimical [hostile] to the liberties of their country...."[28] Then the Continental Congress voted to place the colony under a ban of nonintercourse—meaning that other colonies were not allowed to do business with or correspond with Georgia. In their view, if Georgia was not on the colonies' side, then it must be on England's side and should be treated with the same contempt and mistrust.

This challenge to Georgia's loyalty to colonial interests prompted quick action from its patriot leaders. Within two months a provincial government had been organized, and in July 1774, Georgia notified the Continental Congress that it was ready to join the union. Five delegates were chosen to attend the congress: Archibald Bulloch, Noble W. Jones, John Houstoun, Lyman Hall, and the Reverend John Zubly. Congress promptly removed the ban of nonintercourse.

For the next eighteen months the provincial government and the royal colonial government struggled to gain control over the other. The situation came to a climax in January 1776 when four British warships suddenly appeared in the Savannah port. Suspicious, the provincial government arrested Governor Wright, who later escaped to England on a British vessel. This event ended Britain's royal colonial government in Georgia, at least for a time. The provincial government moved quickly to draw up laws and policies for the newly independent state. Within a year it had developed a new constitution, which provided for one house of representatives, a weak chief executive, and a judiciary dependent on the house.

The War Begins

In April 1775, British troops and colonial militia exchanged fire in Massachusetts, beginning the Revolutionary War. After word of the hostilities reached Georgia, the provincial government there attempted to gather troops and supplies to aid in the colonies' defense. It soon became apparent, however, that Georgia had little manpower to contribute. Despite the population increase of the last decade, Georgia was still sparsely populated compared to the northern colonies and Virginia. Few men could be spared to fight if communities were to survive economically. As a result, Georgia was ill equipped to aid the Continental Army or even provide for its own defense.

The provincial government knew it would need to request troop reinforcements to man the defense of Georgia. As the southernmost

In April 1775 British troops and colonial militia exchange fire at Lexington, Massachusetts, signaling the start of the American Revolution.

colony, bordered by the British territory of Florida, Georgia was in a precarious position. The colony's protection was important to block a British invasion from the south.

In the early years of the war the Continental Congress took steps to defend Georgia by authorizing the southern detachment of the army to invade Florida. Such an offensive action, led by General Charles Lee, would have cut off British invasion by land in the south. However, Lee's troops never made it to Florida because of problems with transportation and a lack of food and supplies.

The Fall of Savannah

Shortfalls in military supplies also had an impact on the defensive effort in Georgia. As the war progressed, requests for more troops to defend the region were either ignored or denied because Continental Army commander George Washington insisted that no soldiers could be spared—the fighting was too intense in the north. Left to its own devices, Georgia could muster few troops for its defense. Savannah had only six hundred troops to protect it, while the militia was scattered throughout the upcountry providing sporadic defense to small communities and farms.

The Button Gwinnett–Lachlan McIntosh Duel

Button Gwinnett and Lachlan McIntosh were colonial leaders in Revolutionary Georgia. Both were on the American side, but also led divisive factions within the patriot ranks. The merchants and planters of the low country made up the

Button Gwinnett led the radical faction made up of mostly upcountry farmers.

conservative faction, led by McIntosh, a Highland Scot who had served in the military as a young man under James Oglethorpe. The more radical faction, made up of mostly upcountry farmers, was led by Button Gwinnett.

The struggle between the two factions was more of a struggle for power between two differing economic groups rather than ideologies. However, Gwinnett and McIntosh also held personal animosities. Although Gwinnett became president of the new state of Georgia in the early years of the war, he highly coveted McIntosh's

In the meantime, the British had sent spies from Florida to report on the military strength of Georgia and the level of loyalist versus patriot sentiment among the people. Discovering the colony's weak military strength and believing exaggerated reports of loyalist sentiments, the British planned to conquer Georgia, restore the royal colonial government, and then work their way up through the northern colonies, pinning Washington's Continental Army between the southern and northern British campaigns.

The first maneuver in the British plan was to attack and seize both Sunbury (another important port town) and Savannah. By doing so position of colonel of Georgia Continental troops.

Their differences came to a head in 1777 after McIntosh's brother George was arrested for suspected loyalist sympathies and treated harshly by the state government, for which McIntosh held Gwinnett responsible. Later, during a floor session of the assembly, McIntosh called Gwinnett "a Scoundrell & lying Rascal." Insulted, Gwinnett challenged McIntosh to a duel, the usual response of an insulted party.

The duel was fought on May 16, 1777. Both Gwinnett

Lachlan McIntosh led the conservative faction of merchants and planters from the low country.

and McIntosh were wounded, but Gwinnett died of his injury three days later, leaving McIntosh the victor. McIntosh was tried by the assembly for murder, but acquitted. Public sentiment was unfavorable to him, and McIntosh left Georgia when Washington transferred his assignment from the Georgia Continental troops to the northern troops of the Continental Army.

they hoped to restore the colonial government and thus make it easier to drum up loyalist support and enthusiasm for taking the upcountry. In December 1778 the British marched on Savannah with two thousand men, who easily subdued the few hundred American troops. Half of the patriot soldiers were killed or captured while less than twenty British soldiers were killed. By December 29 the British had succeeded in taking Savannah and made plans to send Wright back to Georgia to reestablish the royal government.

Within a year, with the aid of the French, American forces attempted to retake Savannah. Unfortunately there was little communication or

The Legend of Nancy Hart

During the savage fighting between patriots and Tories in the Georgia upcountry, an American colonel, John Dooly, was killed by a band of Tories at his home. Later the alleged murderers showed up at the home of Nancy Hart, and Kenneth Coleman retells the story of how she single-handedly subdued the men in his book The American Revolution in Georgia:

"Five of the murderers, says the legend, called soon after their gory deed at the cabin of Nancy Hart in frontier Wilkes County and demanded food. While the food was being prepared, they stacked their muskets in the corner and made merry while emptying a well-filled jug. Nancy sent her daughter to the spring for water and to warn the Whig [patriot] men in the neighborhood that Tories were in the cabin. When the meal began more water was needed, and the daughter was dispatched with instructions to signal the Whigs to come to the cabin. Then Nancy began to slip the muskets through a crack between the logs. The Tories discovered this, but before they could do anything Nancy, musket in hand, warned them that she would shoot the first one who moved. A Tory moved, Nancy fired, and the Tory fell to the floor dead. A second musket was instantly in Nancy's hands and the daughter returned with word that Whig men would arrive soon. Nancy's reputation with firearms was well-known, but her being cross-eyed made it difficult for her prisoners to know just which one she was watching.... Another Tory moved and joined his companion on the floor. The other three accepted Nancy's demand that they 'surrender their ugly Tory carcasses to a Whig woman' and were hanged without further ado when the Whig men arrived."

The legendary Nancy Hart, musket in hand, holds Tories at bay in her cabin.

cooperation between the French commander, Count d'Estaing, and the American commander, General Benjamin Lincoln. As a result the effort failed, with tragic loss of life as one eyewitness during the siege recounted:

> For half an hour the guns roared and blood flowed abundantly. Seeing an opening between the enemy's works Pulaski [a Polish count in the French forces] resolved, with his Legion and a small detachment of Georgia Cavalry, to charge through, enter the city, confuse the enemy, and cheer the inhabitants with good tydings [tidings]. General Lincoln approved the daring plan. . . . Pulaski shouted his men forward, and we, two hundred strong, rode at full speed after him, the earth resounding under the hoofs of our chargers. For the first two moments all went well. We sped like knights into the peril. Just, however, as we passed the gap between the two batteries, a cross fire, like a pouring shower, confused our ranks. I looked around. Pulaski lies prostrate on the ground! I leaped toward him, thinking possibly his wound was not dangerous, but a canister shot had pierced his thigh, and the blood was also flowing from his breast probably from a second wound. Falling on my knees I tried to raise him. He said [something] in a faint voice. . . . At that moment a musket ball grazed my scalp, blinded me with blood and I fell to the ground in a state of insensibility.[29] [Pulaski later died from his wounds.]

Despite the failure of this initial attempt, there were several other tries to retake Savannah during the war. All of them failed.

The fall of Savannah affected the political atmosphere in Georgia, especially in the upcountry where colonists tended to be divided in their loyalties. With Governor Wright restored to power in Savannah, the morale of Tories was boosted and many of them formed bands of their own militia to prey on Whigs and their families. The Whigs of Georgia, however, were equally encouraged by the provincial government, which was still operating in the upcountry, and they also were organized into militia groups.

French-American forces led by Count d'Estaing and General Benjamin Lincoln failed to retake Savannah from British forces in October 1779.

The Tory and Whig militias wreaked violence upon each other in the upcountry. Sometimes men would return from a raid to find their homes burned and families murdered. Other times, families would flee their homes in fear for their lives. Once a band of Whig militia discovered a group of four hundred women and children who were hiding in the woods after escaping attacks on their homes by Tories. They managed to move them to a place of safety in North Carolina. The British army also marched through heavily Whig parishes and burned every farmhouse and all the crops—in Wilkes Parish one hundred estates were destroyed.

However, by the summer of 1781 the Whigs had regained control of the upcountry. This success was partly due to the arrival—finally—of some much needed Continental Army troops, who helped to take back scores of British-occupied posts and helped the militia gain a badly needed victory against the Tories at the Battle of Kettle Creek. By July all of Georgia was in American hands except for Savannah. Soon loyalists began to flee the upcountry, leaving the royal government in Savannah with no way to obtain supplies for regular troops defending the town.

Within a few months the British surrendered to Washington at Yorktown, and plans for the British evacuation of Savannah were under way. Finally, on July 12, 1782, Savannah was under American control again.

Although the Whig forces in Georgia celebrated the end of the war and their hard-won independence, the people and the government of the new state recognized that many difficult years of rebuilding their lives and economy lay ahead. Moreover, they had to face the important question of how Georgia would function as an independent political state—on its own or as part of a larger union.

Chapter Five

Rebirth in the New Union

After the end of the Revolutionary War, Georgia concentrated on rebuilding its economy and formulating its government. With so much property destroyed and thousands of loyalists gone, Georgia faced the difficult task of fostering new growth both in the population and in the economy. Moreover, the state's leaders were confronted with the challenge of creating a system of government that would protect both the rights of freemen and an economy based on slave labor.

Perhaps the greatest postwar change in Georgia, however, was the shift in who controlled the state's leadership. The war had destroyed the aristocracy that had just begun to emerge, and the provincial government of the war years had consisted primarily of frontiersmen from the upcountry—the so-called common people. After the war they retained their power, and the upcountry influence gave rise to greater democracy, addressed the needs of common people, and made its mark in the political, social, and economic systems of postwar Georgia.

Political Changes

The influence of the independent frontiersman not only affected government policy but also changed the way the political system was organized. Prior to the war there existed no form of local government—all political acts were vested in the colonial government at Savannah. After the war the upcountry individualists insisted on having more control over local affairs. Parishes had become counties during the war (via the provincial government) and during the 1780s the counties were regulated by a sheriff and a commissioner who was responsible for overseeing the construction and maintenance of county roads. Soon towns were also establishing their own governments, beginning with Savannah. The town commissioner controlled public property, oversaw sanitation concerns and the police, and collected local taxes.

While local governments were able to address some of the more minor legislative issues, they were forced to turn to the state government when it came to getting economic aid. Immediately after the war ended, Georgia had to find a way to help its residents whose farms had been destroyed and who had no way to make a living or feed themselves until after the 1782 crops had been planted and harvested.

The city of Savannah in 1778. Savannah was the first town in Georgia to establish its own government.

One way the state government thought it could raise money to aid its citizens was by selling the property of former Tories. The Confiscation and Banishment Act of 1782 called for the confiscation of Tory property, which would be auctioned off to pay the state's war debts. Although many properties were confiscated and sold, they did not bring in as much revenue as hoped.

By 1784 the government saw that proceeds from confiscated property would not be enough to settle all its financial obligations. As a result the Georgia legislature levied a property tax to supplement its income, and thereafter the government relied on various domestic and import taxes, license fees, and sales of western lands in addition to confiscated property for its income.

Georgia wanted to obtain more western land because such an asset would give it a rich financial resource. Not only could it sell land to pay its expenses, but land could be used to compensate war veterans and the families of soldiers killed. During the 1780s land bounties of 250 acres were granted to veterans, with no obligation to pay property taxes for ten years. Moreover, the children of military officers or soldiers who had died in distinguished service to the Revolutionary cause were granted from 500 to 1,000 acres each.

Ironically, the sale and settlement of western land actually created another big problem for the state government. These lands were inhabited mostly by Creek Indians, who had already ceded large tracts of land to Georgia in the decade just prior to the war. Although many were not eager to cede yet more land, smaller native groups led by subchiefs sometimes signed treaties ceding land to Georgia without having the proper authority to do so. Georgia held that such treaties were valid even though the leading Creek chiefs disputed their legality. Often, settlers who made their home on disputed land became targets of Indian reprisals. Moreover, many frontiersmen and their families, called squatters, settled on Creek lands without government approval. This so angered the Creeks that they began raiding white settlements in the western parts of Georgia without regard for whether their targets were squatters or legal settlers. Thus the settlers on the western frontier began clamoring for military aid to protect them from the Creeks.

Tensions with the Creeks escalated throughout the 1780s, leaving the government extremely concerned about the state's military forces, which continued to be inadequate. This concern eventually played a major role in the state's support of a strong national government, which Georgia's leaders believed would be necessary to protect the state in case of war with the Indians.

The government did attempt to make major treaties with the Creeks in order to prevent disputes, but the natives were able to circumvent making agreements through the brilliance of one of their leaders, Alexander McGillivray, a shrewd negotiator. Despite McGillivray's success at preventing the further cession of Creek lands, frontiersmen continued to move west and settle illegally. Eventually the rights of the Creeks were overshadowed by the need for these lands to help rebuild Georgia's economic vitality.

Economic Changes

The new government of Georgia worked hard to design economic policies that would bring renewed prosperity. Since about half the private property in Georgia had been destroyed, with much of it abandoned, the government provided some relief to those farmers who needed help and time to rebuild their farms. It also needed to attract more people to live in Georgia, since about three thousand upcountry farmers had fled Georgia and a roughly equal number of slaves had been transported out of the state.

Georgia also pursued foreign trade markets with France, Britain, and the West Indies, hoping to regain some of its prewar commercial prosperity. During the war, trade in Georgia had almost come to a standstill because of the destruction of plantations and civil violence in the upcountry region. After the war, these markets for goods still existed but production was rather poor. While the main trade commodities continued to be rice, lumber, naval products, and some tobacco, the poor condition of coastal plantations in the early 1780s led to sparse rice crops. Indigo ceased by 1789 to be a trade good in Georgia, since Britain had almost exclusively been the importer of this crop, and after the war Britain no longer imported indigo from Georgia.

Perhaps the greatest problem for the Georgia economy, however, was the disruption of the slave labor system. During the war many slaves disappeared due to the absence of their owners or because the estates where they lived had been destroyed by the military. Some escaped and joined Indian tribes while others managed to make it to the Caribbean, where they established their own communities. Others were seized as property by the armies of either side and forced to build fortifications or transport supplies. Immediately after the end of the war the state government confiscated slaves from Tory estates and sold them for payment of war debts. Many planters returned to their ruined plantations to find few, if any, of their slaves still present. Without slave labor the plantations could not exist.

During the 1780s a few slaves were imported and gradually the economy began to grow again. However, rice never did regain its prominent prewar status. This may have been partly due to the development of a new invention that would revolutionize the Georgia economy during the 1790s.

The Birth of King Cotton

Prior to the 1790s cotton had never been considered very profitable because of the painstaking labor involved in handpicking it and

Eli Whitney invented the cotton gin, revolutionizing Georgia's economy.

separating the cotton fibers from the seeds. In 1793 a young tutor from Connecticut named Eli Whitney visited a cotton farm near Savannah. After observing the process needed to clean the seeds from the cotton, he invented a device that could clean seeds fifty times faster than a person could by hand. He called his device the cotton gin.

The cotton gin revolutionized Georgia's economy. With the tremendous decrease in labor and time needed to clean the cotton, the crop

With the invention of the cotton gin, large cotton plantations sprang up in Georgia, and the slave population grew.

became increasingly profitable. All over the state cotton plantations sprang up and with them, Georgia's slave population grew. Because the inland areas as well as the coastal regions were suited for cotton production, many upcountry farmers prospered. They built and operated large cotton plantations powered by slave labor as the rice plantations of the low country once had been. Within the first decade after the invention of the cotton gin, cotton production increased by twenty times. The slave population also went up, jumping from about 59,000 in 1800 to over 149,000 in 1820.

Social Changes

In addition to becoming more economically powerful, upcountry people also exerted more influence in education and religion in post-war Georgia. Prior to the war, the budding aristocracy had controlled the government and therefore the education and religious leadership of the colony. Usually only the most privileged plantation families could afford to either send their children away to school or hire a private teacher at home. The rise of the common people in the upcountry and their influence in state politics meant that educational and religious policies would be changed to reflect their needs.

The provincial government had abolished the Church of England as the established church in 1777, and throughout the war years religious observances and church attendance were at a low. Although Anglican congregations continued to exist in Georgia, the influence of the church declined as many of the clergy and church members—many of whom were Tories—left the colony. In addition, pressing economic concerns often took precedence over religious issues.

However, during the 1780s the churches of the upcountry settlers, Baptist and Methodist, emerged as the dominant religious denominations in Georgia. Historian Reba Strickland explains how religion played a role in Georgia society:

> It seems reasonably certain that a large number, but not a majority, of the Anglicans remained loyal to the Crown. Although many Highlanders and Scotch-Irish were loyalists, most of the Presbyterians were rebels [patriots]. Probably all ... Midway Congregationalists [Methodists], Baptists and Jews were patriots. The Lutherans were split, but the majority appear to have favored independence. The Quakers were loyal or at least neutral. Except for the latter, it appears that all the dissenting sects tended to favor liberty and those which, in Europe or America, had suffered religious persecution were most ardent in their support of the American cause. Indeed, this seems to have been a much stronger controlling factor than economic interests in determining the side to which individuals gave their allegiance.[30]

Since the American side was victorious in the war, it followed that those church groups that were most strongly patriotic would also emerge as the new dominant religious sects in Georgia.

Like religion, education also declined during the war years. What schools there were in Georgia ceased to exist except for a few in Savannah. Despite this decline the groundwork for a state public school system was laid out by the provincial government in 1777: "Schools shall be erected in each county, and supported at the general expense of the state...."[31] After the war, each county was authorized

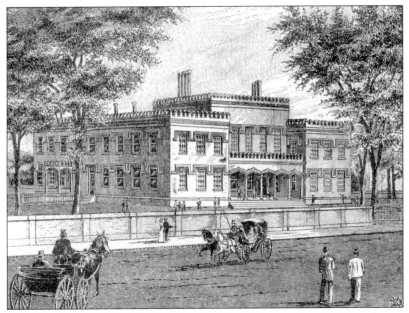

The Georgia state public school system started with the opening of Richmond Academy (shown) in April 1785.

to obtain one thousand acres of land for the purpose of selling it and then using the funds to erect free schools, hire teachers, and purchase school supplies. The first such school was Richmond Academy in Augusta, which opened in April 1785 in a brand-new building. Several other counties opened schools in the late 1780s.

Some upcountry parents began to recognize the need for a basic education for their children. Many communities established crude schools, located on worn-out tracts of land, called Old Field Schools. The curriculum of these schools rarely went beyond basic reading, writing, and arithmetic. These frontier schools held short terms and sometimes had rather low standards for hiring teachers. George Gilman, who attended an Old Field School as a child, remembered one of his teachers:

> There was no school in the Goose-Pond neighborhood, on Broad River, from its first settlement in 1784 until 1796. The first teacher was a deserter from the British navy, whose qualification was, that he could write. He whipped according to navy practice. On cold mornings, when fire could not be

conveniently had, he made the children join hands and round and round, whilst he hastened their speed by the free application of the switch. [32]

In addition to county academies and Old Field Schools, Georgia also intended to establish a state university. Under the guidance of Governor Lyman Hall and upcountry representative Abraham Baldwin, the university was organized. Baldwin noted that there was no school of higher education south of Virginia. He also thought it a disservice to send Georgia's youth out of the state or the country to get an education full of foreign ideas and prejudices (often prejudices existed between states). This view is evident in this act of the Georgia legislature in 1785:

[Education should] encourage and support the principles of Religion and Morality, and . . . place the Youth under the forming hand of society, that by Instruction they may be moulded to the love of Virtue and good order. Sending them abroad to other Countries for their Education will not answer these purposes, is too humiliating an acknowledgement of the ignorance or inferiority of our own, and will always be the cause of so great foreign attachments, that upon principles of policy it is not admissible. [33]

Baldwin was a major force behind the drawing up of a charter and setting aside of land for the construction of the university. He thought a commonsense approach would be more valuable to Georgians than a classical curriculum, and emphasized instruction in "the principles and rudiments of language, more particularly of the English; the ready and exact use of numbers; some of the first principles of Geography, History, Mensuration [measurement], [including equipment such as] a Pair of Globes, and some small part of a Philosophical apparatus." [34] Such a curriculum is evidence of the strong influence of the common people in educational policy.

Despite enthusiasm for the project, financial delays did not allow the university to open until 1801. Part of the reason for the delay was the weakness of Georgia's state government. Political leaders realized that Georgia needed help to strengthen itself economically and defensively—and it needed a strong national government as a source of support and resources.

Role in the Constitutional Convention

Despite the fierce individualism and new political clout of the upcountry settlers, opinions were divided over whether or not to support a strong national government. While many Georgians felt a strong central authority was necessary to provide them with the military support they needed, others feared losing control at the state level—especially regarding slavery.

These issues were debated during the Constitutional Convention in 1787, where delegates from each state came together to create a national government satisfactory to everyone. One thing the delegates from Georgia—William Few, Abraham Baldwin, William Pierce, and William Houstoun—agreed on was that Georgia needed the protection of a union of states above all else, as constitutional scholars Christopher Collier and James L. Collier explain:

> Georgia had a variety of concerns at the Convention, among them fear of northern attempts to end slavery and to cut up its huge western area into additional states. Overriding everything, however, was the fact that Georgia bumped up against the Spanish south and west [Florida had been returned to Spain after England lost the Revolutionary War] and was exceedingly vulnerable to attack. The Spanish were supplying the local Creek Indians with arms, ammunition, and sanctuaries in Florida. Unless the state got help from the North, an alliance of Spanish and Creeks could easily overrun Georgia's 25,000 inhabitants. . . . The very lives of Georgia's citizens depended on a firm union with the other states . . . isolated, the state was doomed. [35]

Baldwin and Pierce were the most ardent supporters of a strong central government, but all of the Georgia delegates wanted to protect the rights of the states because they did not think a central government could adequately decide matters of local importance—primarily the matter of slavery. Thus in the early days of the convention the Georgia delegation formed an alliance with the other Deep South states (North and South Carolina) and the three biggest states (Virginia, Pennsylvania, and Massachusetts). The southern states promised to support the big states on issues of importance to them, and in exchange the big states promised not to harass the southern states on the issue of slavery.

Abraham Baldwin disintegrated this alliance for reasons vital to Georgia's interests. During the convention the delegates split over the issue of proportional representation—whether representation in Congress would be based on the population of each state. The Big Three–Deep South alliance favored proportional representation because the larger populations of the Big Three would give them a majority of representatives in Congress as well as an advantage when addressing their needs. However, the smaller states were adamant that at least one house of Congress be based on an equal number of representatives from each state. Otherwise, they feared, the interests of the smaller states would be ignored in favor of those of the larger states. The debate was so fierce that delegates from the smaller states threatened to walk out of the convention if they did not get equal representation in one house. If that happened, the convention would be a failure and the union would not occur.

Therefore, when the vote was held on the issue of representation, Baldwin voted against proportional representation rather than for it as his comrades in the alliance had. Luther Martin, a delegate from Maryland, recounted Baldwin's action in a speech:

Abraham Baldwin was for a strong central government but wanted to protect the rights of the state to decide local matters.

Georgia had only two representatives on the floor (the other two were attending a session of Congress), one of whom (not, I believe, because he was against the measure, but from conviction, that we [the small-state delegations] would go home and thereby dissolve the convention, before we would give up the question) voted also in the negative, by which that State was divided. Thus . . . the convention being equally divided, five States for the measure, five against, and one divided, there was a total stand, and we did not seem likely to proceed any further. At length, it was proposed, that a select committee should be [chosen], composed of a member of each State, which . . . should endeavor to devise some mode of conciliation or compromise.[36]

The compromise that resulted was that two senators would represent each state in the upper house (the U.S. Senate), while population would determine the number of each state's representatives in the lower house of Congress (the House of Representatives). In the end, by breaking the alliance, Baldwin saved the convention and preserved Georgia's interests.

The Fourth State in the Union

After the convention ended, the proposed Constitution was sent to Georgia and the other states for ratification. Georgia called a convention for this purpose, and twenty-four delegates from all but one of the state's counties attended. The delegates debated the Constitution for only one day before voting unanimously to approve it. Recognizing the threat of war with the Creeks and the Spanish because of the growing tensions of the 1780s, the delegates wasted no time ushering Georgia into the Union. On January 2, 1788, Georgia became the fourth state of the Federal Union.

Although Georgia had early recognized its need to be part of a strong union, in the decades that followed, the issue of states' rights gradually overshadowed this need. The growth of the cotton industry after 1793 and the slave labor that accompanied it was largely responsible for this shift in priorities. Moreover, by the 1830s the last of the Indians were forcibly removed to Oklahoma Territory, and

Abraham Baldwin

Abraham Baldwin never gave a reason for why he voted against the other Georgia delegate (four represented Georgia but only two were present at this particular debate) during the debate on proportional representation, thereby saving the Constitutional Convention from failure. However, it is apparent that his decision was influenced heavily by his personal background.

Baldwin was born and raised in Connecticut, the son of a self-educated blacksmith. He later studied theology at Yale, where he became a tutor and chaplain (religious official of the college). Interestingly, when Baldwin was only thirty he was offered the prestigious position of professor of theology at Yale, which he turned down. At this point Baldwin decided to study law and was admitted to the Connecticut bar in 1783.

Wishing for greater opportunity, Baldwin decided to leave Connecticut, where there was an abundance of lawyers. He settled in the Georgia upcountry and established his law practice among the frontier farmers. He preferred working with the common people, who owned few if any slaves and were more closely tied to his own background. In addition, the scarcity of lawyers in the upcountry made business good for a young lawyer just starting out.

Baldwin, a moderate in political thinking (neither radical nor conservative, but in between), became very popular among the upcountry farmers. After only three years in his new state, he was selected a member of the Georgia delegation to the Constitutional Convention. At the convention, Baldwin's familiarity with the New England states and the Connecticut delegates gave him an understanding of the needs and concerns of that region—an understanding that most southern delegates did not have. He also understood that if the convention voted to have proportional representation in both houses, the small states would definitely walk out. If that happened, a strong union would not be formed and Georgia would be left vulnerable. Baldwin sacrificed a lesser interest in order to preserve the interests of his state.

Florida was eventually ceded to the United States, leaving Georgia free of the threat of invasion.

By the 1860s, Georgians no longer felt the need to be part of a union that threatened an institution they felt was necessary to their economic security. The northern states, with their greater population, controlled the national government and wanted to end slavery in the South. The Southern states, including Georgia, believed that a national government controlled by the North could not represent their interests. They argued that they had the right to legally protect matters important to their states. The issue of states' rights caused Georgia and other Southern states to secede from the Union, resulting in the Civil War. In a way, Georgians were simply acting as they always had, against the grain of authority, just as the earliest settlers had resisted the trustees' authority when they concluded the government no longer served their needs.

Notes

Introduction: Georgia's Legacy
1. Kenneth Coleman, *Colonial Georgia: A History.* New York: Charles Scribner's Sons, 1976, p. xiv.

Chapter One: Precolonial Times: Conflict and the Struggle to Dominate Georgia
2. Quoted in Rodney M. Baine, ed., *The Publications of James Edward Oglethorpe.* Athens: University of Georgia Press, 1994, pp. 249–50.
3. Quoted in Spencer B. King Jr., *Georgia Voices: A Documentary History to 1872.* Athens: University of Georgia Press, 1966, p. 1.
4. Quoted in King, *Georgia Voices,* p. 2.
5. Quoted in King, *Georgia Voices,* p. 5.
6. Quoted in King, *Georgia Voices,* p. 4.
7. Quoted in Elmer D. Johnson and Kathleen Lewis Sloan, *South Carolina: A Documentary Profile of the Palmetto State.* Columbia: University of South Carolina Press, 1971, p. 73.
8. Coleman, *Colonial Georgia,* p. 6.

Chapter Two: Establishing the Colony: A Noble Experiment
9. Quoted in Baine, *The Publications of James Edward Oglethorpe,* p. 66.
10. Quoted in King, *Georgia Voices,* p. 8.
11. Quoted in Coleman, *Colonial Georgia,* p. 20.
12. Quoted in E. Merton Coulter, ed., *The Journal of Peter Gordon.* Athens: University of Georgia Press, 1963, p. 31.
13. Quoted in Ira L. Brown, *The Georgia Colony.* New York: Macmillan, 1970, pp. 21–22.
14. Quoted in Brown, *The Georgia Colony,* pp. 22–23.
15. Quoted in Brown, *The Georgia Colony,* p. 25.
16. Quoted in Coulter, *The Journal of Peter Gordon,* p. 26.

Chapter Three: Changes in Daily Life in Colonial Georgia
17. Quoted in King, *Georgia Voices,* pp. 178–79.
18. Coleman, *Colonial Georgia,* p. 139.

19. Quoted in King, *Georgia Voices*, p. 114.
20. Quoted in King, *Georgia Voices*, pp. 42–43.
21. Quoted in King, *Georgia Voices*, pp. 47–48.
22. Quoted in King, *Georgia Voices*, p. 8.
23. Quoted in Brown, *The Georgia Colony*, p. 62.

Chapter Four: The Revolution and Georgia's Civil War

24. Quoted in Kenneth Coleman, *The American Revolution in Georgia*. Athens: University of Georgia Press, 1958, p. 3.
25. Quoted in King, *Georgia Voices*, p. 53.
26. Quoted in King, *Georgia Voices*, p. 55.
27. King, *Georgia Voices*, pp. 50–51.
28. Quoted in King, *Georgia Voices*, p. 58.
29. Quoted in King, *Georgia Voices*, pp. 69–70.

Chapter Five: Rebirth in the New Union

30. Quoted in Coleman, *The American Revolution in Georgia*, p. 177.
31. Quoted in Coleman, *The American Revolution in Georgia*, p. 225.
32. Quoted in King, *Georgia Voices*, p. 207.
33. Quoted in King, *Georgia Voices*, p. 205.
34. Quoted in Coleman, *The American Revolution in Georgia*, p. 228.
35. Christopher Collier and James Lincoln Collier, *Decision in Philadelphia: The Constitutional Convention of 1787*. New York: Ballantine Books, 1986, pp. 171–72.
36. Quoted in King, *Georgia Voices*, pp. 76–77.

Chronology

1540
Hernando de Soto explores the Georgia region.

1566
First Spanish fort established on St. Catherines Island in Guale (now Georgia).

1702
Last Spanish residents withdraw from Guale to Florida.

1732
King George II of Great Britain grants a charter to the trustees for establishing the colony of Georgia; James Oglethorpe and the first colonists bound for Georgia leave England on the *Ann*.

1733
Savannah is established at Yamacraw Bluff on the Savannah River.

1739
War of Jenkins' Ear begins between England and Spain.

1742
Oglethorpe defeats the Spanish at the Battle of Bloody Marsh.

1751
Trustees give up the charter and Georgia becomes a royal colony.

1760
James Wright becomes the third and last royal governor of Georgia.

1775
Provincial government forms in Savannah.

1776
Governor Wright is arrested but flees Georgia for England by ship.

1778
Savannah is captured by the British.

1782
British evacuate Savannah.

1788
Georgia ratifies federal Constitution and becomes the fourth state in the union.

For Further Reading

Tracy Barrett, *Growing Up in Colonial America*. Brookfield, CT: Millbrook Press, 1995. This book discusses education, training, and leisure activities for children growing up in the American colonies.

Joyce Blackburn, *James Edward Oglethorpe*. New York: Dodd, Mead and Company, 1970. A detailed look at Oglethorpe's life from childhood to his death in 1785, it includes interesting information about his motivations for founding the colony and how he felt about Georgia during the royal period, the Revolutionary War, and the immediate postwar years.

Ira L. Brown, *The Georgia Colony*. New York: Macmillan, 1970. A chapter by chapter look at the colony's founding and education, work, social life, and immigrants during its first two decades. It also includes chapters on the Spanish invasion of the 1740s and the royal period, including information on the three royal governors of Georgia.

Ruth Dean and Melissa Thomson, *Life in the American Colonies*. San Diego, CA: Lucent Books, 1999. This comprehensive book covers topics such as daily life in the cities and rural areas of the colonies, typical employments, immigrants, changes in political, religious, and social attitudes, and relations with the Native Americans.

Dennis B. Fradin, *From Sea to Shining Sea: Georgia*. Chicago: Childrens Press, 1991. The author includes a brief section on the exploration and colonial history of Georgia. This reference also includes a gallery of famous people from the state, a map, and a historical timeline.

Bobbie Kalman, *Colonial Life*. New York: Crabtree Publishing, 1992. Brief information and dramatized photographs describe colonial homes and towns, family life, play and school for children, men's and women's fashions, travel, and life for a slave family.

Zachary Kent, *America the Beautiful: Georgia*. Chicago: Childrens Press, 1988. Here readers will find information on the land, people, and culture of Georgia, including a section with interesting anecdotes on colonial history.

Bonnie L. Lukes, *Colonial America*. San Diego, CA: Lucent Books, 2000. This comprehensive look at the development of the American colonies includes a chapter on the settlement and colonial history of Georgia.

Works Consulted

Books

Rodney M. Baine, ed., *The Publications of James Edward Oglethorpe.* Athens: University of Georgia Press, 1994. This comprehensive compilation of Oglethorpe's published writings includes reports to Parliament on the conditions of three English debtor prisons. It also includes articles on Georgia and South Carolina that describe the region and its native peoples.

Harry J. Carman, Harold C. Syrett, and Bernard W. Wishy, *A History of the American People: Volume 1 to 1877.* New York: Alfred A. Knopf, 1960. This comprehensive text offers in-depth information on the settlement of the colonies, the development of a colonial economy, intercolonial conflicts, and changes in the political and religious climate in colonial culture. It also discusses the process of creating the federal Constitution.

Kenneth Coleman, *The American Revolution in Georgia.* Athens: University of Georgia Press, 1958. This book provides an in-depth study of the reasons why Georgia joined the Revolution, the Whig-Tory political and military fighting in the upcountry, and details of both the restored royal government and provincial government that coexisted from 1780 to 1782.

Kenneth Coleman, *Colonial Georgia: A History.* New York: Charles Scribner's Sons, 1976. This comprehensive book provides information on the precolonial history, founding, and early years of Georgia. It includes extensive information on Indian relations, agriculture, the lifestyle in colonial Georgia, economics, and the development of upcountry farmers' political power during the Revolutionary War.

Christopher Collier and James Lincoln Collier, *Decision in Philadelphia: The Constitutional Convention of 1787.* New York: Ballantine Books, 1986. This is an in-depth look at how the Founding Fathers developed the federal Constitution. It provides insight into the motivations of the individual delegates who framed the document and pieces together how these various factors contributed to the final work.

E. Merton Coulter, ed., *The Journal of Peter Gordon.* Athens: University of Georgia Press, 1963. This journal is actually a 1738 recounting by Gordon as he remembered the preparations and journey to Georgia, the founding of Savannah, and its early years until 1735. He presents an interesting discussion of why the colonists felt the trustees' rules were unfair, especially the property regulations.

David Hawke, *The Colonial Experience*. New York: Bobbs-Merrill Co., 1966. This book provides a comprehensive look at the reasons for colonial settlement and also discusses the politics, society, economy, and religion of the colonies.

Elmer D. Johnson and Kathleen Lewis Sloan, *South Carolina: A Documentary Profile of the Palmetto State*. Columbia: University of South Carolina Press, 1971. A source for primary quotes from historical documents and personal letters and journals related to South Carolina history.

Paul Johnson, *A History of the American People*. New York: HarperCollins, 1997. This in-depth look at the early settlement and colonial era of the United States includes informative sections on colonial politics at all levels and the development of the colonies' independence from England.

Spencer B. King Jr., *Georgia Voices: A Documentary History to 1872*. Athens: University of Georgia Press, 1966. Here readers can get detailed information on the history, education, government, economy, and society of Georgia up to the Reconstruction years. Each section is supported with primary quotes relating to the subject.

Michael Kraus, *The United States to 1865*. Ann Arbor: University of Michigan Press, 1959. This author explores the motivations behind settlement of the colonies, with brief sections devoted to Georgia, and the political and social changes of the mid-1700s that led to the war for independence.

Index

Picture Credits

Cover: Hulton-Getty/Archive Photos/Courtesy of the Georgia Historical Society

Archive Photos: 66, 71

Bettman/CORBIS: 49, 51, 56, 59, 63

Chris Jouan: 9, 17, 19

CORBIS: 36, 37, 68

The Georgia Historical Society: 10, 26, 33, 39, 42, 53, 57, 64, 65, 77, 80

Hulton-Getty/Archive photos: 27, 34, 43

North Wind Picture Archives: 13, 16, 18, 29, 74, 75

Stock Montage, Inc.: 21, 23, 46

About the Author

Christina M. Girod received her undergraduate degree from the University of California at Santa Barbara. She worked with speech- and language-impaired students and taught elementary school for six years in Denver, Colorado. She has written scores of short biographies as well as organizational and country profiles for educational multimedia materials. The topics she has covered include both historical and current sketches of politicians, humanitarians, environmentalists, and entertainers. She has also written several titles for Lucent Books, on subjects such as Native Americans, entertainers, Down syndrome, learning disabilities, and *Connecticut*, also part of the Thirteen Colonies series. Girod lives in Santa Maria, California, with her husband Jon Pierre and daughter Joni.